STUDIES IN SOCIOLOGY

Edited by Professor W. M. Williams
University College, Swansea

14   Sociology and Social Welfare

STUDIES IN SOCIOLOGY

1 *The Sociology of Industry*
   by S. R. Parker, R. K. Brown, J. Child and M. A. Smith
3 *Demographic Analysis*
   by B. Benjamin
4 *The Family*
   by C. C. Harris
5 *Community Studies*
   An Introduction to the Sociology of the Local Community
   by Colin Bell and Howard Newby
6 *Social Stratification*
   An Introduction
   by James Littlejohn
7 *The Structure of Social Science*
   A Philosophical Introduction
   by Michael Lessnoff
8 *A Sociology of Organisations*
   by J. E. T. Eldridge and A. D. Crombie
9 *The Sociology of Leisure*
   by Stanley Parker
10 *A Sociology of Friendship and Kinship*
   by Graham A. Allan
11 *The Sociology of Women*
   An Introduction
   by Sara Delamont
12 *Introducing Social Statistics*
   by Richard Startup and Elwyn T. Whittaker
13 *The Family and Industrial Society*
   C. C. Harris
14 *Sociology and Social Welfare*
   by Michael Sullivan

Sociology and Social Welfare

MICHAEL SULLIVAN
University College, Swansea

London
ALLEN & UNWIN
Boston   Sydney   Wellington

Allen & Unwin, the academic imprint of

Unwin Hyman Ltd
PO Box 18, Park Lane, Hemel Hempstead, Herts HP2 4TE, UK
40 Museum Street, London WC1A 1LU, UK
37/39 Queen Elizabeth Street, London SE1 2QB

Allen & Unwin Inc.,
8 Winchester Place, Winchester, Mass. 01890, USA

Allen & Unwin (Australia) Ltd,
8 Napier Street, North Sydney, NSW 2060, Australia

Allen & Unwin (New Zealand) Ltd in association with the Port
Nicholson Press Ltd,
Private Bag, Wellington, New Zealand

First published in 1987

British Library Cataloguing in Publication Data

Sullivan, Michael
    Sociology and social welfare. – (Studies
    in sociology; 14)
1. Social service – Great Britain
I. Title   II. Series
361'.941   HV245
ISBN 0–04–301213–2
ISBN 0–04–301214–0 Pbk

Library of Congress Cataloging in Publication Data

Sullivan, Michael.
    Sociology and social welfare.
(Studies in sociology; 14)
Bibliography: p.
Includes index.
1. Public welfare – Great Britain.   2. Welfare state.
3. Social service – Great Britain.   4. Great Britain –
Social policy.   I. Title.   II. Series: Studies in
sociology (George Allen & Unwin); 14.
HV245.S85   1987   361.6'1   86–17294
ISBN 0–04–301213–2 (alk. paper)
ISBN 0–04–301214–0 (pbk.:alk. paper)

Set in 10 on 12 point Bembo by Columns of Reading
and printed in Great Britain
by Billing and Son Ltd, London and Worcester

Contents

	Acknowledgements	viii
	Introduction	ix
1	*The Context of Welfare*	1
2	*Perspectives on the Modern British State*	29
3	*Approaches to Welfare*	62
4	*The Development and Functions of Social Work*	103
5	*State, Welfare and Social Work*	130
6	*Sociological Imagination and the Practice of Social Work*	155
7	*Sociology and Social Welfare: Problems and Prospects*	168
	Bibliography	176
	Index	188

Acknowledgements

Professor W. M. Williams first suggested that I should write this book after hearing a conference paper on which the last chapter is loosely based. My debt to him does not, however, end there: his presence along the corridor has been a continuous spur to complete the work more or less on time despite an ever-increasing teaching load; he has made very constructive comments on earlier drafts; and his swift reaction to the final draft of my manuscript minimized pre-submission anxiety levels.

Other debts need acknowledgement. Paul Wilding, first as teacher and then as senior colleague at University College, Cardiff, contributed largely to my social science apprenticeship. He acted as encourager, exemplar and intellectual stimulator. I hope this book, whatever its deficiencies, is some small repayment of his devotion of time, kindness and intellectual skills. The support of colleagues, and the incisive, if sometimes unwelcome, comments of students in the School of Social Studies at Swansea are gratefully acknowledged. Ken Davies, a postgraduate community work student in my sociology and social policy lecture series also deserves thanks. He identified, in a piece of written work, additional problems which needed to be grappled with in the writing of Chapter 5.

Edna Owen, Vera Quinn and Caryl Johnstone struggled personfully and happily with various and increasingly messy drafts of the manuscript. They have my thanks.

Finally I should acknowledge the contribution of Sue Sullivan and of my stepson Ben Dipper to the completion of this book. Sue lived with my uncertainties, helped clarify my thinking and was, despite her own doctoral work, *usually* longsuffering about my sometimes non-existent contribution to an already unequal division of domestic labour. Ben spent a number of evenings making good various bibliographic inadequacies. Other and remaining inadequacies in the text are, of course, my responsibility.

Michael Sullivan
Swansea
April 1986

Introduction

Britain in the 1980s is, according to some commentators, a society in the grips of a process of fundamental social change. Radical right Conservative governments have, it is claimed, redrawn the boundaries of state involvement in civil society. Nowhere, it is argued, are these changes more evident than in contemporary attempts to roll back the state from involvement in welfare. This book is, in part, an attempt to understand the nature and scope of these apparent changes by contextualizing the study of welfare within a wider sociological analysis of state and society in postwar Britain.

Wright Mills, writing in the context of an American society in the throes of social change as far back as the 1950s, has suggested that to understand more fully the confusing collective and individual experiences of a society in transition there is a need for a quality of mind which he calls 'the sociological imagination'.

> It is not only information that they [i.e. those seeking to understand the social world] need . . . It is not only skills of reason . . . What they need and what they feel they need is a quality of mind that will help them to use information and develop reason in order to achieve lucid summations of what is going on in the world and what may be happening to themselves. (Mills, 1959)

One of the most significant claims of this book is that the theory and practice of welfare would gain much if its activities were informed by the sociological imagination. That imagination prompts us to move behind the taken-for-granted assumptions, the commonsense understandings of everyday life in order to search for the meanings of the 'inner life and external careers' of individuals or groups of individuals. One of the most important concerns of this book is, therefore, to suggest how a sociological quality of mind might influence the development of a conscious and reflective approach to welfare practice and theory. If state social work has developed what Bailey calls a 'theoryless practice' rooted in what Wright Mills has seen as an 'incapacity to rise above a series of cases', then that practice may tend to be uncritical, unreflective and deeply embedded in the commonsense understandings of dominant, if changing, social ideologies. As a consequence, the provision of welfare may become little more than a mechanism for perpetuating the social, economic and political relations of an inegalitarian capitalist society.

In order more fully to understand the role and functions of welfare in contemporary society it is necessary to develop a set of critical awarenesses: of the social, economic and political context of state provided welfare; of the way in which social processes contribute to, and sometimes mould, intra-group, intra-family and intra-psychic conflicts; and of the limits and possibilities of autonomous action in welfare. To this end the book is concerned to address a number of issues which might help us to explore understandings of the social realities of welfare.

Chapter 1 sets the provision of welfare services, and other post-war state interventions, in recent historical context. In so doing it poses the question: 'Why should the state have become involved in systematic social and economic intervention – of one sort or another – in the recent historical period?'

Chapter 2 seeks to provide a range of answers to this question by devoting itself to an exposition of various explanations of state intervention in civil society in the period since the Second World War. As such, it presents explanations drawn from Marxist sociology, the literature of social democracy, the political theory of the 'radical right' and the economic and social theory of the 'industrial logic' school.

Chapters 3 and 4 apply these varied understandings to the development and functions of state welfare, in general, and state social work, in particular. This exercise leads, in Chapter 5, to the promotion of an argument that state welfare activities are constrained but not entirely determined by a ruling class or elite sections of it. The argument is developed to suggest that, although the state itself, and the welfare policies developed by it, reflect – in most historical periods – the interests of a powerful class or elite, sufficient relative autonomy from those interests exists within the state and state agencies to allow the critical welfare worker to work both 'in and against the state' and in the interests of the clients of welfare.

Chapter 6 represents an attempt to address this particular product of the sociological imagination to instances of state sanctioned social work practice.

It is, however, also a contention of this book that the discipline of sociology which has, to a large extent, danced coyly on the margins of the applied social studies field would also gain from a more intimate liaison with social welfare practice. As readers will see, the concluding chapter of this book is concerned not only to itemize the benefits sociology can bestow on social work but also to suggest benefits for sociology itself. British sociology, much of which still seems preoccupied with either blue book empiricism or macro-level theory generation might find in the practice of social work an arena to test the social utility of sociological theory.

The pages that follow, then, represent an attempt not only to construct a social work practice rooted in a self-conscious, critical and sociological imagination about welfare but also to point up the importance of a practice informed process of theory generation in the sociology of welfare.

This book might therefore be found useful by a variety of audiences: the social worker or other welfare practitioner wishing to understand the nature, possibilities and context of state welfare. prctice; the sociologist interested to set the state provision of welfare within a wider analysis of social, political and economic processes; and the general reader wishing to understand more fully the often confusing world of social welfare.

1 The Context of Welfare

What we now regard as the British Welfare State – the provision by the state of benefits and services in the areas of education, health, income maintenance, housing and personal social services – has a relatively short history. It was established in the 1940s with the implementation of a package of government policies which heralded state intervention on a much larger scale and in a more systematic way than ever before. A national health service was created with the intention of providing a universal health care service free at the point of use. Compulsory secondary education, sanctioned by the 1944 Education Act, was introduced with the stated purpose of equalizing the educational opportunities of children from different social classes. A system of income maintenance, drawing largely on the philosophy outlined in the Beveridge Report (Beveridge, 1942) took the place of the less significant social insurance schemes of the early twentieth-century Liberal governments, and was seen by many as the instrument by which poverty would be eradicated. The state replaced private charities as the main provider of personal social services, and intervened in the provision of housing in a way undreamt of before the Second World War. (Useful factual summaries of the development of the welfare state can be found in Sked and Cook, 1979; Marwick, 1982.)

Throughout the following three decades intervention in welfare increased in scope and momentum despite small scale opposition particularly in the Conservative Party (see MacLeod and Powell, 1952). The foundations of the welfare state were built upon by succeeding governments. Welfare state expansion took place throughout the extended period of postwar economic growth in Britain and even in the early years of economic retrenchment. Welfare statism could be seen as a

reflection of the politics of consensus practised during this
period by both major political parties (Marshall, 1965,
pp. 180–1; Marshall, 1975, p. 105).

During the 1950s investment in council housing – and the
number and quality of properties built – reached new heights.
In the 1960s following the publication of the Robbins Report
(Robbins, 1963) higher education was made available to a
wider section of the population than had hitherto been the case.
This was achieved by means of capital expenditure and
consequent recurrent expenditure on new universities and by
the introduction of academic ability as the sole relevant
criterion governing university entrance. In the mid 1960s a
further major state intervention in education occurred: the then
Labour government introduced a system of comprehensive
secondary education to replace the discredited bipartite system
which had been in operation since the 1940s. New elements
were introduced into the income maintenance system: an
earnings related unemployment benefit in 1966 and a state
earnings related pension scheme in 1975, for instance. Personal
social services were integrated, expenditure increased and their
responsibilities widened following the passage of the Local
Authority Social Services Act (1970) and the Children and
Young Persons' Act (1969). Housing controls and subsidies
were introduced throughout the whole period, and the
National Health Service, while being the subject of reorganization and review, was also the object of constantly increasing
state finance.

In the thirty years following the end of the Second World
War large scale intervention by the state in social welfare
formed part of the political orthodoxy of both major political
parties. State welfare became woven into the fabric of everyday
life to such an extent that Jones and Novak could claim that
'for large clusters of people . . . life from the womb to the
grave is monitored by, or is dependent upon, a vast network of
state social legislation and provision' (Corrigan, 1980, p. 143).

At the time of writing, however, controversy rages about
whether the apparent consensus on large scale state intervention
in welfare has been shattered (Mishra, 1984; Taylor-Gooby,
1985). Some (Hall, 1979; Leonard, 1979) have suggested that

cuts in welfare expenditure since the mid 1970s and the restructuring of the welfare state promised and to some extent implemented by the Thatcher governments constitute a fracture in the postwar settlement on welfare. More than this, they argue conflict over state welfare has been fuelled by a radical right manifesto for a minimalist, non-interventionist state. State intervention in welfare, as in industry and the economy, is to be substantially removed and the market, rather than the state, is to regulate economic relations and provide services. The state is to be rolled back in welfare and in other areas of social and economic life (Conservative Party, 1979; 1983).

Others have argued that such an analysis overlooks the continuities and overstates the discontinuities in state interventionist policies over the last decade (Sullivan, 1984; Taylor-Gooby, 1985). Some regard the Conservative governments of 1979 and 1983 as embarking on 'the greatest experiment in social intervention we have ever seen' (Elis Thomas, 1985). The state, it is argued, may be intervening in welfare and elsewhere in different ways and with different aims than hitherto. Nonetheless, the diminution of state control is not one of those aims.

In this atmosphere of intellectual controversy and political bewilderment the various models and perspectives which have been used to explain state intervention in social welfare have, again, come under scrutiny (Taylor-Gooby and Dale, 1981; George and Wilding, 1985; Taylor-Gooby, 1985) Indeed, the following three chapters of this book contribute to the process of understanding the complexities of our contemporary social world. Too often, however, state welfare has been studied in what can only be called a sociological vacuum. Despite recent attempts to understand state intervention in welfare in the wider context of general state activities (Gough, 1979; London Edinburgh Weekend Return Group, 1980; Taylor-Gooby and Dale, 1981; Mishra, 1984), welfare state studies demonstrate, on the whole, a failure to relate the history and practice of the state in welfare to the history and practice of the state in other areas of social and economic life. In an attempt to locate state welfare in this wider context, to illuminate the shifts – real or apparent – in political ideologies of welfare and to explain the nature of contemporary state intervention in welfare, this chapter and the next are devoted to two tasks. The first of these is to review major state interventions in social and economic life in Britain over the last forty years. The second is to provide a range of sociological models of the state which seek to explain – and sometimes prescribe – state activity in this period.

Features of the Postwar British State

Prelude: the War Years

If most, and arguably all, of the postwar period has been characterized by large scale state intervention in civil society, then the war years themselves were a harbinger of the interventionist future. The exigencies of war prompted a degree of central planning and control of industry and economy unusual in British society. The war effort was seen to require the central direction of production. A war economy severely curtailed the production of luxuries. Disruption of imports and of indigenous food and clothing production necessitated the introduction of rationing and controls (Addison, 1982, pp. 130–1, 161–2) The British state at war claimed to require economic sacrifices from all sections of the population. To effect such sacrifices required state intervention.

During wartime the state intervened in the control of industry in a way it had never done before. Under the Emergency Powers Act (1940), the government sought and got powers to regulate working hours and conditions and to enforce the settlement of pay claims through a process of bipartite negotiation involving employer and employee representatives (Harris, in McLennan, Held and Hall, 1984). Such was the change in levels of state intervention that one social historian has claimed that the 'direction and control of life and labour were probably more total (and more efficient) than in any other country save for Russia' (Marwick, 1974, p. 151).

The wartime coalition government also signalled its intention to intervene more systematically than previous governments in the provision and control of social welfare. The seeds of the welfare state may be said to have germinated during this period. Despite some parliamentary opposition from Conservatives, the philosophy of full employment and social security enunciated in the Beveridge Report was largely accepted (Addison, 1982, pp. 223–4). Additionally, plans for a national health service (Willcocks, 1967) and for the introduction of compulsory secondary education (Rubinstein and Simon, 1973) were developed and, in the latter case, enacted before 1945.

Consensus, for whatever reasons and however fragile, was forged around a package of interventionist policies during the war years. Whether such a consensus was one shared by all sections of British society or merely by political leaders and senior state personnel is, of course, an open question. One thing is certain: interventionism in the war years set the scene for what was to follow.

1945–75: Three Decades of Interventionism

State intervention in the social and economic life of British society was a constant and increasingly marked feature of the thirty years which followed Labour's landslide victory in the 1945 general election. Interventionism was accepted as an important feature in the management of the democratic socialism of the Attlee government, of Churchill's Tory democracy, of the age of affluence associated with the Macmillan governments, the technological revolution of the first two Wilson governments and the pre-social contract years of the early 1970s. Throughout this period Britain witnessed significant state activity in areas which had in earlier periods substantially, if not exclusively, escaped the guiding hand of state regulation and control. This more systematic intervention by the state can be illustrated by a consideration of economic and social policy since the war, to which we now turn.

ECONOMIC POLICY 1945–75

Despite changes of government in 1951, 1964 and 1970, continuities in economic policy can be clearly discerned during

this period. These continuities seem particularly marked in
three areas: the organization and control of industry; the
philosophy of economic management; and the practice of
economic management.

THE ORGANIZATION AND CONTROL OF INDUSTRY

In a famous speech marking the end of the Second World War
on 15 August 1945, the new Labour Prime Minister – Clement
Attlee – pledged his government to work for economic
recovery and social justice. These goals were to be achieved
through a process of transforming rather than destroying
British capitalism. The organization of industry was seen as a
crucial arena for state action in the postwar transformation of
British society and the British economy. Central state control
of key industries was seen as essential if the government's twin
aims were to be achieved. Consequently, the postwar Labour
government set about creating a mixed economy where public
and private enterprise coexisted alongside each other. Certain
major industries were nationalized during this period: civil
aviation in 1946, coal in 1947, cables and wireless and transport
in 1947, electricity in 1948, gas in 1949, and steel in 1951.
Although the Conservative governments of 1951–64 did not
themselves nationalize further industries, and indeed de-
nationalized steel in 1953, little if any attempt was made to alter
the balance of the mixed economy. Indeed the attitude of
Conservative governments of the period to the organization of
industry may be sensed in the words of Macmillan – Prime
Minister for part of the period – as creating 'a capitalism which
incorporates socialism' (Barker, 1978, p. 132). Further nationalization occurred during Labour's occupancy of government,
1964–70. British Aerospace and British Shipbuilders were
nationalized during this period and steel was renationalized in
1967.

The nationalization of key industries, the creation of a mixed
economy and consequent administrative changes in this period
represented major state intervention in an area of the economy
where it had been almost wholly absent until the 1940s.
Nationalization, however, was simply an important, rather
than an exclusive, mechanism for state intervention in the

organization and control of industry during this period. Especially in the middle and latter years of this thirty year span, other methods of direct intervention were used. By the early 1960s it had become evident that, despite nationalization and other government interventions in the economy (which we discuss later), economic growth in Britain was proceeding at a slower pace than had been hoped or than pertained in other industrial societies.

Furthermore a process of rapid technological development was occurring in the developed industrial world. With the stated aim of fuelling the fires of technological revolution in British industry, other direct interventions by the state in industry were introduced. Again, as we shall see, consensus between the political parties on state intervention in the economy in this period, spanning the 1960s and early 1970s, was evident despite differences in political emphasis.

In 1966, the then Labour government introduced the Industrial Reorganization Corporation, which was empowered to use government capital to promote and develop industrial enterprise. As such it played a direct part in the modernization and reorganization of a number of industries including the nuclear industry, the electrical industry and the motor industry. In 1964 the same government created a new Ministry of Technology, and its work was aided in 1968 by the introduction of the Industrial Expansion Act, which aimed to encourage technical and scientific innovation in industry. Key aims here were the modernization of the machine tool industry and the promotion of Britain's computer industry. The state at a central level, then, was involved in direct intervention in the control and organization of British industry and its involvement during this later period was not limited to those public corporations which it or its predecessor Labour governments had created through nationalization.

It is interesting to note that, although the 1970 Conservative government disbanded the Ministry of Technology and abolished the Industrial Reorganization Corporation, it reinforced state involvement and intervention in the organization of industry at a direct level. It created the Department of Trade and Industry to co-ordinate commercial and industrial policies, and introduced, in 1972, the Industry Act. This Act gave the state more extensive powers of intervention in industry than it had possessed before and was supplemented by the creation of an Industrial Development Unit to implement industry policies and an Advisory Board to give advice.

The establishment of the National Enterprise Board by a Labour government in 1975 and the concomitant passage of yet another Industry Act permitted further extensive and direct intervention in the private sector of British industry. The National Enterprise Board (a government holding company) provided extensive financial incentives to private industry in part as inducement to rationalize, modernize and reorganize.

State intervention in the organization and control of industry in the three decades following 1945 was, then, one feature of the state's involvement in areas hitherto regulated and controlled by the market.

State involvement in the organization and control of industry appears throughout the whole period to have operated within a party political consensus on its necessity and acceptability. State intervention in industry seems to have been predicated on a philosophy of economic management shared by both major political parties.

THE PHILOSOPHY OF ECONOMIC MANAGEMENT

Until the Second World War the state played a comparatively small role in the management of the economy. Major manufacturing industries, like minor ones, operated within a capitalist market economy where the profit motive and the price mechanism more or, more often, less successfully regulated economic exchange. The economic depression of the inter-war years took place within the context of such a market economy, as did the economic recovery of the late 1930s, albeit aided by demand for arms and by cheap raw materials and privileged credit arrangements from the colonies and Sterling Area (Harris, in McLennan, Held and Hall, 1984). From 1940 (and particularly from 1945), however, the market economy principle was replaced by a philosophy of economic management which presumed and encouraged the intervention of the

British state in the control and management of the economy. This new philosophy was to guide government policy and intervention into the mid 1970s and was based on the idea of demand management of the economy. Some commentators see, in this development, a major transformation of the British State (Jessop in Scase, 1980, p. 28).

In simple terms, successive governments in the period 1945–75 made attempts at macroeconomic management of the economy in order to maintain it at an optimum level. Governments in this period intervened to fine tune the economy so that the twin dangers of unemployment and inflation could be avoided and steady economic growth achieved.

So the 1945 settlement included a commitment to large scale state intervention in the economy, a commitment to use state apparatuses to regulate the level of aggregate demand in the economy. A number of instruments could be and were used by governments in the post 1945 period to achieve this end. In periods where the economy was in an apparently uncontrolled upward surge, governments acted to depress the economy. So, for example, at times when production levels were rising rapidly consequent difficulties of rising inflation and shortage of labour were also likely to occur. By macroeconomic intervention the state could and did act in such periods to reinstate equilibrium in the economy. Traditional features of the dampening down process included: increasing levels of taxation which would act to decrease demands for products and restrain economic activity; increases in interest rates which had the effect of restricting credit and thereby restraining investments in industry; and the consequent regulation of inflationary pressures resulting from capital inflows into the economy.

Similarly when the economy was in slump government could and did intervene by means of state apparatus to stimulate demand. Taxation levels would be decreased to leave more money in the economy thereby encouraging consumption. Interest rates would be reduced to encourage investment in industry and to stimulate consumer expenditure. (A helpful synopsis of the mechanisms of demand management can be found in McLennan, Held and Hall, 1984, pp. 93–4.)

For roughly three decades this Keynesian principle of demand management of the economy apparently worked well enough. Though it did not eradicate slump–boom cycles in the economy it certainly mitigated their effects: between 1952 and 1964 average unemployment in Britain was only 380,000 and by 1973 it had risen to only 590,000. Discussions of the reasons for the relative success of Keynesian economic principles in practice during this period abound (see McLennan, Held and Hall, 1984, pp. 94–103) as do explanations of its ultimate failure (McLennan, Held and Hall, 1984, pp. 206–8). What is important here is that for a period of about thirty years political consensus (at least between parties of government) existed. That consensus made possible, and made real, extensive state involvement in the control of the economy in order to maintain full employment and economic growth. The period is characterized by almost continuous interventions by state and government in economic management based on an economic philosophy unacceptable before 1940 and increasingly unpopular, in Britain and the USA at least, after 1975.

These three decades of significant state involvement in the British economy were characterized, then, by large scale involvement in the control and organization of industry and by an underarching, interventionist policy of macroeconomic management. They were similarly characterized by what some (Middlemas, 1979, pp. 389–429) have seen as the extension of the state by means of the incorporation of both sides of industry in economic planning functions.

ECONOMIC PLANNING AND INCORPORATION

Postwar Britain saw the creation and maintenance of a mixed economy. The state became involved in the economy at a number of levels: it took control of some industries creating a public sector of industry; it developed a framework for and agencies to assist the reorganization of industry to keep pace with technological and other changes; it attempted to fine tune the economy to provide a context in which a modern mixed economy could flourish and provide high levels of employment. To ensure the success of a strategy for continued and controllable growth in the British economy, however, implied not only that the state should intervene in the structure of the economy and industry but also that it should intervene to incorporate British industry into the state and into the management of the economy. In free market capitalism those who owned capital and those who sold labour were competing forces. In state interventionist mixed economy Britain, attempts were made to modify that relationship so that they would, in some senses, be partners with each other and government in ensuring the continued prosperity of the British economy. If the continued profitability of industry and the maintenance and improvement of workers' living standards were seen as dependent, in part, on the successful intervention of the state in industry, then the limits of success were seen, by successive governments, as dependent on industry's ability and willingness to be part of a tripartite relationship (including industrial management and owners, trade unions and government) initiating and co-ordinating economic policy. Governments formed by both political parties established forums for the planning and management of the economy in which tripartite involvement was of a formal or informal nature. In 1962 the Conservative government established the National Economic Development Office (NEDO). Its task was to gather information and make recommendations over a wide range of economic policy and planning. Part of the NEDO structure were National Economic Development Committees (NEDDY's) which consisted of economic ministers, trade unionists and industrialists.

In 1964, the newly formed Labour government established a short-lived Department of Economic Affairs. The DEA was charged with developing an indicative plan for economic growth and, unlike the Treasury with which it vied as an initiator and co-ordinator of economic policy, its deliberations consistently, if informally, included both sides of industry.

Tripartite co-operation, formal and informal, successful and unsuccessful was initiated by governments during the 1960s and 1970s on the issues of prices and incomes and industrial relations – both seen as crucial to the management of a growth economy. The National Board for Prices and Incomes (1965)

and its successors the Pay Board and the Price Commission
(1972) all involved the widest representation of interests. The
Commission on Industrial Relations (1969), which functioned
to conciliate between employers and trade unions, had similar
representation. Following the abandonment of the White
Paper, *In Place of Strife*, in 1969 the Trades Union Congress took
on quasi-government functions in intervening in industrial
disputes. During the Social Contract years (1974 on) government, employers and the Trades Union Congress acted in
concert (despite discordant notes and later deafening cacophony
from individual trade unions) to plan for wages and prices in an
economy that had become sluggish and in which unemployment was a growing and worrying problem (Robertson and
Hunter, 1970, pp. 189–202).

These examples, together with the growth of quasi-
autonomous non-governmental organizations such as the
Manpower Services Commission – set up in 1974 to develop
plans for labour market policy despite its role since 1979 as
masseur of unemployment figures – illustrate the extension and
penetration of the state in the 1960s and 1970s into previously
autonomous areas and agencies of civil society. The state
attempted, with some success, to incorporate previously hostile
combatants as partners in the state (or quasi-state) machinery
(Middlemas, 1979, pp. 430–63).

SOCIAL POLICY 1945–75

Following the Second World War, the activities of the state in
Britain were massively increased. An interventionist state
emerged to replace a liberal, largely non-interventionist state.
The interventionist state was characterized by two major
features: the large scale and consistent economic intervention
we have considered above, and the extension of welfare policies
and creation of a welfare state which we consider now (and, in
more detail, in Chapter 3).

That the state should intervene in a systematic way to
provide and control welfare was, before the Second World
War, a highly contentious proposition – even Keynes argued
that the state should act only to provide those services which

people could not provide for themselves (Marwick, 1974). But the consensus of the war years on welfare appears to have continued into the peace and the welfare state was created and expanded, more or less consistently until the mid 1970s. Continuity rather than political schism marked state involvement in welfare during this period. The apparently linear progression of welfare state expansion can be illustrated by a consideration of welfare state policies of the period. In this section we concentrate on three areas of provision which illustrate the points to be made: income maintenance and social security provision, education and the National Health Service. Detailed accounts of policy development and implementation in these areas exist elsewhere (e.g. Hall, Land, Parker and Webb, 1978; Held, 1982; McLennan, Held and Hall, 1984). What interests us here is the steady and apparently consensual rise of state welfare during this period.

INCOME MAINTENANCE AND SOCIAL SECURITY PROVISION

The income maintenance and social security system has often been regarded as the foundation stone of the welfare state. W. H. Beveridge is, with a large degree of justice, credited as its originator and as founding father of the British Welfare State. It is, of course, the case that social security provisions had existed since the early twentieth century. Nonetheless, the scheme promoted by Beveridge (and substantially implemented by the postwar Labour government) extended and in some crucial respects transformed earlier schemes. The scheme that resulted from the 1946 National Insurance Act, the National Insurance Industrial Injuries Act and the 1948 National Assistance Act was intended to provide financial benefits to cover earnings interruptions for those insured. It was therefore to include benefits to cover periods of sickness, unemployment and maternity. It was to provide benefits to widows and orphans, the old, the industrially injured and to offer a funeral grant to rescue the poor from the perceived indignity of a pauper's grave (George, 1973, pp. 34–6). The scheme was universal in its coverage and based on the principle of insurance. Individuals contributed to the scheme while in work and they and their families benefited from it at times of earnings interruption. Originally the scheme yielded flat rate benefits generated largely by flat rate contributions. National Assistance at a subsistence level was provided for those who, for one reason or another, were ineligible, or ceased to remain eligible for National Insurance Benefits.

The income maintenance and social security system did not remain unchanged over the thirty year period under consideration. The flat rate contribution/benefit principle was abandoned in 1966 when an earnings related unemployment benefit was introduced. This benefit was based on an earnings related contribution and was introduced with the stated aim of acting as a cushion against frictional unemployment during a period of industrial rationalization. New non-contributory benefits were introduced: family income supplement in 1971; a non-contributory invalidity benefit in 1974; and a child benefit scheme introduced in 1977 despite lukewarm support (Land, 1978; Field 1978). Other changes, reflecting the material realities of postwar Britain, also occurred. Principal among them were the relatively large numbers of claimants subsisting for long periods of time on a National Assistance/ Supplementary Benefit scheme intended as a short term safety net scheme for a small minority of claimants. Nonetheless, continuity in social security policy was more significant than change. Both Labour and Conservative governments kept faith with the basic Beveridge principles, even in later periods when general taxation came to subsidize a greater proportion of spending in a system expanded in scope and supporting larger numbers of people (owing to economic and demographic factors). As late as 1973 and 1974 Social Security Acts underwrote the Beveridge principles despite making peripheral changes and, sometimes, improvements in provision. (For a history of this period, see Kincaid, 1973; Hall, Land, Parker and Webb, 1978.)

Throughout this period, then, state involvement and increasing state expenditure formed the basis of maintaining and expanding, however *ad hoc* that expansion, the British income maintenance and social security system. Growth in state social expenditure rates in this area remained substantially, if not totally, unquestioned by governments formed by both major political parties. A bipartite political consensus on the place of social security in postwar British society, and on the growth of that system to respond, even if unsuccessfully, to changes in the economy, appeared to exist throughout the period. That basic commitment, if not the system's administration, remained substantially unchanged until the Social Security Reviews of the mid 1980s.

EDUCATION

Continuity and growth were also the main features of state provision and policy in education during this period. That the state should intervene to provide a universal system of secondary education had been established as a bipartisan political principle in the mid 1940s. Despite seemingly significant divisions within the Labour Party in the 1950s (and between the Labour Party and the Conservative Party throughout that whole period) over the organization of secondary schooling, the development of comprehensive education and the involvement of state agencies in setting the agenda for change was marked by a breadth of consensus. This consensus in Westminster certainly and possibly in British society at large belies the apparent significance of conflict over the issue (Parkinson, 1970; Rubinstein and Simon, 1973; Fenwick, 1976).

The expansion of higher education (referred to above, p. 2) and of teacher training and of further education – all bringing with them increased state expenditure and increased state involvement in planning education – was presided over by governments of both political persuasions (cf. Kogan, 1971, for a discussion of developments in higher education policy).

It is of course true that even during this period differences did exist on where the limits of state involvement in education should be set. The Conservative governments of the period were more committed than Labour governments to the retention of a private sector in secondary education, for example (Parkinson, 1970, pp. 94–118).

Similarly Labour governments have been more receptive, in principle if not in practice, to the idea of merging the misnamed private sector of higher education (universities) with the completely state controlled (albeit local state) public sector to form a unified tertiary sector of education. However, despite these differences a large measure of agreement has characterized attitudes to state involvement and expenditure in education during this period.

THE NATIONAL HEALTH SERVICE

Although the National Health Service was born amidst tremendous conflict over the nationalization of health (see Foot, 1975, for an account of this conflict) there existed, during the period we are presently studying, a surprising degree of political accord over its continuation. Although its creation was fiercely resisted by the Conservative opposition of the time, the 1951 Churchill government's ready acceptance of continued state intervention in health care led one of his contemporaries to quip that he had 'stolen the socialists' clothes while they were bathing'. State involvement in health was never seriously questioned by governments of this period and there was considerable agreement between the political parties over the reorganization of the NHS in the early 1970s. Like income maintenance and education (and indeed like housing and the personal social services) the principle of state intervention and control in health appeared sacrosanct during this period.

It is interesting to note, however, that unlike any of the other areas of provision the NHS operated for the whole of this period with what might be termed a within-service mixed economy. That mixed economy – embracing private provision in NHS hospitals and the partial use of the price mechanism for most of the period by means of prescription, optician service and dental charges – also, interestingly, received bipartisan political support (the Labour Party in government and in practice, if not in principle, operated the mixed economy of health).

So, whereas the other areas of provision studied demonstrate a seeming consensus on state intervention and wholesale state funding, the National Health Service in operation during this period demonstrates a consensus on state intervention with mixed funding. Indeed the National Health Service in the years 1948–75 might be seen as a microcosm not only of the state's interventionist activities in welfare but also of its operation of a mixed economy.

In summarizing the argument so far, then, we may conclude the following:

(1) The thirty years following the Second World War were marked by a change in the nature and growth in the scope of state intervention in the social and economic life of British society.

(2) This state intervention in civil society was sanctioned by succeeding governments, both Conservative and Labour and grew out of a consensus – at least at the level of political leadership – which, in effect, transformed the state.

(3) The activities of this 'transformed state' were developed around the twin commitments of succeeding governments to a mixed economy and the intervention of the state in social welfare.

The extent to which such consensus on the growth of the state was embraced by a wider constituency than that of government is one of the problematics considered later in this book. We move now to consider the apparent breakdown of this consensus in the years following 1975 – another problematic which we will attempt to address later in the chapter.

1975–85: the 'Rolling Back' of the State and the End of Consensus?

In 1979 a Conservative government, under the leadership of Mrs Margaret Thatcher, was elected. Its manifesto for that and the 1983 general election and its policies in government have been argued to draw extensively on the work of economists, philosophers and social scientists of the radical right (Hayek, 1944; Friedman, 1962; Powell, 1969; Joseph, 1972; 1976). The policies of Thatcher's governments have been characterized as 'Powellism in government' (Barnett, 1984), nursed and developed into maturity by Sir Keith Joseph acting in the role of ideological commissar. The principles on which Thatcher's conservatism are said to be based are threefold:

(1) a need to reduce drastically government expenditure as the public sector is seen as a burden on wealth creating sectors of the economy;

(2) a firm control of the money supply in order to restrain inflation;

(3) a reduction or confinement of the role of government simply to the maintenance of conditions in which free markets may function properly.

Put quite simply, it is the enunciation of these principles and their partial, if not complete, transformation into government policies which have led to the promotion of the idea that the British state, after three decades of interventionism, is being 'rolled back' or withdrawn from interference in the affairs of civil society. As we will see, changes have occurred in the relationship between state and civil society during this period. An apparent consensus, however limited or extensive, has been apparently shattered. The aims of government in this period have apparently been quite different from those of governments in the earlier period, as witnessed by the following proposition by Joseph and Sumption:

> the aim must be to challenge one of the central prejudices of modern British politics, the belief that it is the proper function of the state to influence the redistribution of wealth for its own sake. (1979, p. 232)

Our goal of explaining state intervention in the post-1945 period – apparent consensus on growing state intervention, followed by apparent rupture of that consensus – will however be most aided not by a study of statements of intent but by a consideration of empirical realities. It is therefore to those realities that we must now move.

Prelude: the Early 1970s

As early as the beginning of the 1970s the postwar settlement
on economic and social intervention appeared vulnerable.
Although the political rhetoric of government was still couched
in terms of repairing rather than challenging that settlement,
policy changes were occurring which appeared to be portents
of a fundamental shift in the role and functions of the British
state. The Heath Conservative government (1970–4) flirted
with post-Keynesian economics and a reduction in state activity
in the economy. The Wilson government (1974–6) appeared to
abandon, on election, the commitment to full employment on
which the postwar settlement had been built (Riddell, 1983). It
was in the years following 1975, however, that the interventionist state *appeared* to be 'undergoing an abrupt and
fundamental reversal of its whole direction' (Taylor–Gooby
1985, p. 12).

1975–9: the Winds of Change?

This short period of time is also a particularly interesting one.
For these four short years a Labour government presided over
an economy apparently sliding into reverse. Unemployment
rates were rising alarmingly, if not as spectacularly as in the
early 1980s: inflation at times seemed apparently uncontrollable.
(For a contemporary account of the period see Sked and Cook,
1979, ch. 12.) Economic crisis followed economic crisis and
industrial conflict reached new heights culminating in the
'winter of discontent' of 1978–9 when the trade union
movement rejected government policies, particularly those on
wage restraint, aimed at dealing with Britain's economic crisis.
If there has, indeed, been a fundamental shift in the nature and
scope of state intervention in British society, then this period
may be regarded by later commentators as a period of
transition from a consensus on state involvement and growing
state expenditure to one in which fundamental conflict
characterized the debate on the role of the state in civil society
and the degree of economic intervention and expenditure
acceptable in a modern society. Riddell, commenting on this

period argues 'if there has been a Thatcher experiment it was launched by Dennis Healey' (1983, p. 59).

During this period government policies on state expenditure and on state involvement in industry and the public sector of the economy seem to have reflected, on the one hand, a commitment to the interventionist state which had been the political commonsense of the post-1945 period. On the other hand, economic policies also appeared to include elements which portended a future reduction in state activities.

Throughout this brief period, the Labour government attempted to implement Keynesian or neo-Keynesian economic policies to hold down unemployment. It also sanctioned and encouraged increased intervention by the state into other areas of economic management. In particular, the development of a 'social contract' between government and trade unions amounted to state intervention to control pay and prices and was, arguably, the high-tide mark of the interpenetration of state and civil society in Britain. In effect, at least for a short period, government and state offered, and the trade union movement (or at least its leaders) accepted, the role of a quasi-state agency, monitoring and, where possible, controlling increases in pay. On the other hand, it was the Labour government of this period which introduced an economic strategy part of which was governed by monetarist principles. This development is amply described and analysed in a number of excellent texts (especially McLennan, Held and Hall, 1984) but appears to have consisted of the following features:

(1) attempts to control the money supply (first introduced in 1975);
(2) attempts to reduce public expenditure, or at least to halt its rise;
(3) application of cash limits to public spending and to curb the Public Sector Borrowing Requirement.

These monetarist policies undoubtedly led to a reduction in state provision in welfare services as in other services and have been seen as paving the way for private provision and privatization even if that were not the political intention. (Sullivan, 1984.)

Some have argued that the monetarism of the Labour government in the mid to late 1970s should be seen as a politically expedient response to external pressures, prime among them the requirements of the International Monetary Fund in granting Britain a loan during the sterling crisis of 1976 (Riddell, 1983, p. 59).

They point to the 'uncertain mix of policies' (Riddell, 1983, p. 60), to monetarist policies juggled alongside incomes policies and measures to hold down unemployment. They contrast such an eclectic mix with the straightforward monetarism of the later Thatcher governments. Be that as it may, the winds of change in attitudes to state intervention had started to blow in the late 1970s. Whether they precipitated a sea change in state activity in the 1980s is quite another question.

1979–85: the Rhetoric and Reality of the New Conservatism

In May 1979 a Conservative government was elected in Britain apparently pledged to political philosophies and practices quite different from those of the governments of the postwar consensus period. The new Prime Minister and her senior colleagues presented a programme of change for Britain which had been developed over some years and which owed much to the writers of the radical right. The aim of the 'new conservatism' was to shatter what was seen as the postwar consensus on state interventionism, mixed economy and welfare or, in the words of one Thatcherite, to reject the 'false trails of Butskellism' (Lawson, 1981) and to create a new consensus based on quite different principles. Deliberate attempts were to be made to shift the frontiers between the public and private sectors of the British economy, to introduce policies which would stimulate private enterprise and to encourage the creation of a strong private sector in welfare. The proposed principles which would guide policy-making were regarded by the new government – and by many contemporary writers (Leonard, 1979; Hall, 1979; Gamble, 1979; 1980) – as the antithesis of previously dominant consensus principles. Specifically these new guiding principles included:

(1)   a commitment to large scale state intervention in social and economic life being replaced by a commitment to a market economy (Howe 1983);

(2)   a commitment to the authority of the state being replaced by a commitment to the rule of law (Howe 1983);

(3)   a commitment to large scale state intervention in welfare being replaced by a commitment only to a *residual* welfare state (Boyson, 1971; Joseph, 1976; Seldon, 1977; Seldon, 1981).

Political orthodoxies about the relationship between the British state and civil society appeared to have been cast aside. The 'new conservatives' diagnosed the state control and/or regulation of industry, industrial development and industrial relations as having sapped the initiative of private entrepreneurs and as having led to economic decline. Industry and economy needed to be freed of the fetters of state controls and subject only to the regulation of the market. The economic system, if it were to generate wealth and freedom, needed to be developed around the principle of voluntary exchange.

The growth of the state, and particularly the growth of welfare bureaucracies, protective legislation and the like had elevated the authority of the state over people's lives to unacceptable proportions (Powell, 1969). The new conservative proposals included ones concerned with severely limiting the state's paternalistic role and reinstating the rule of law as the primary institution regulating social and economic life (Howe, 1983).

The erstwhile political orthodoxy – of large scale state provision and control of welfare – was also to be challenged. The 'nanny-state' was to be rolled back. Responsibility for the provision of welfare was to be put back in its rightful place – with the individual, the family and the community – and large areas of welfare provision were to be privatized (Conservative Party, 1979).

In short, the new conservatives at the beginning of the 1980s promised a transformation of the relationships between state and society – a transformation that was to be based on the economic principle of sound money and the moral principles of individual freedom and individual responsibility. In their analysis, consensus, state interventionist Britain had created a coercive state in an attempt to redistribute income, wealth and life chances. That coercive state had, at one and the same time, destroyed freedom and the economic growth which was the precondition of redistribution. The new order – based on a sense of personal responsibility, a concept of community self-help and on a concept of individual rather than collective justice (Griffiths, 1983, p. 7) – presumed, in contrast,

> a certain kind and degree of inequality . . . If society wants to preserve economic freedom it cannot predetermine equality which can only be achieved by coercion and therefore against freedom. (Griffiths, 1983, p. 9)

So, if this was the rhetoric of change, what were the empirical realities of Britain in the early 1980s?

The State and Civil Society in the 1980s

It is not the intention here to look at the success of the policy strategies of the Thatcher governments, either in their own terms or in the terms of others. That task has generated a literature of its own (Bosanquet, 1983; LeGrand and Robinson, 1984; Taylor-Gooby, 1985).

What interests us here is to consider whether the empirical realities of new conservative government have changed the relationship between state and civil society in fundamental ways. Certainly the role of the state in the economy has appeared to change. Consistent efforts have been made to control the money supply, large scale privatization has occurred (see Labour Party Research Department, 1985) and the state, in theory, if not in practice, has disengaged itself from a role in industrial relations. Early policies betokened a shift from the postwar consensus on state involvement in industry.

For example, the reduction of the top marginal rate of tax on earned income from 83 to 60 per cent, and of basic rate income tax from 33 to 30 per cent, together with the introduction of a higher threshold for the investment income surcharge in the

1979 Budget can be seen as an attempt to reintroduce incentives for *private* entrepreneurial activity by allowing greater profit for producers of products and greater disposable income for the consumer.

The reduction of public spending and the removal of some capital taxes, pay, price and dividend controls can similarly be seen as contributing to 'shifting the frontiers' between state and the economy and making conditions more amenable for the market.

Additionally, throughout the six years of Thatcher Conservative government up until 1985, state control of industry was curtailed through the denationalization or privatization of many major industries (see McLennan, Held and Hall, 1984, pp. 291–4). The state was apparently moving out of important sectors of the economy to be replaced by corporate, if not yet private, entrepreneurs.

Competition within the public sector and between the public and private sectors was introduced by the imposition of cash limits and other curbs on public spending. Remaining state enterprises were subject, as a result, to continual pressure to improve levels of efficiency and productivity (see Joseph, 1976; Maude, 1977; Redwood and Hatch, 1982; Thompson, 1984).

The welfare state has also been affected by the policy initiatives of the new conservatives. Welfare state services have been affected by straightforward cuts and by the restructuring of services.

Public expenditure restrictions introduced by the Conservative governments of this period have affected welfare services administered by local government as central government has reduced its grant aid to local authorities and introduced measures to curb local expenditure (Labour Party Research Department, 1985). The effects of such an economic strategy on services have been serious.

In local authority education services there have been cuts in equipment and staff. In the Personal Social Services reductions in service have most often occurred in areas of provision where local social services departments have discretionary rather than statutory obligations (for example, in aids and adaptations for the elderly and disabled). Further cuts appear to have occurred in areas of provision, such as the care and control of children, the elderly and disabled where statutory obligations can be fulfilled, at least in theory, without wholesale recourse to residential care.

The effects of financial stringency on housing have been dramatic. Housing cuts have meant that completions in local authority housing have dropped from 130,000 in 1976 to 40,000 in 1982. Rent rises have meant that rents have increased in real terms by over 70 per cent in the same period (Taylor-Gooby, 1985).

Services administered nationally have also been affected by the policy strategies of the so-called new conservatives. Spending on the National Health Service has failed to keep pace with increased demands (Labour Party Research Department, 1985) and has led to real cuts in services. In the field of income maintenance, the removal of the Earnings Related Unemployment Benefit in 1982 not only increased the financial hardship of the unemployed but also gnawed away at the universal state insurance policies of the Beveridge and post-Beveridge generations. The proposed curtailment of the State Earnings Retirement Pension Scheme (established as late as 1977) together with the other changes recommended by the Social Security Reviews of 1984/5 have been seen as an attempt further to shift the boundaries of state involvement in welfare provision.

The privatization of erstwhile state welfare services and the introduction of or increase in charges for service has also appeared to transform the relationship between the state and civil society in welfare. The sale of council houses, pay beds in the National Health Service and the Assisted Places scheme in education have all changed the balance between public and private welfare provision (LeGrand and Robinson, 1984). Sharp increases in charges for some personal social services, for dental, optical and prescription services, have also occurred. However, if we look a little closer at the empirical realities of state involvement and expenditure in society during this period two sets of paradoxes or contradictions, which will need to be explained later, are uncovered. The first concerns the scope of state intervention in welfare during this period, the second concerns state intervention in a wider context.

(i) RHETORIC V. REALITY

A number of commentators (e.g. O'Higgins, 1983; Sullivan, 1984; Taylor-Gooby, 1985) have questioned whether the continuities in state involvement and expenditure in welfare pre- and post-1979 are not, in fact, stronger than the discontinuities. Taylor-Gooby has argued that, despite the heady rhetoric of the Thatcherites, the new conservative state has not moved out of welfare to anything like the extent that might have been expected. Indeed, he argues that, notwithstanding the cuts in services outlined above, the trend of postwar increases in social expenditure has been stabilized rather than reversed during this period. The major discontinuity in policy which he can discern is that the new conservatives have used unemployment as a social policy, thus driving a wedge between the employed and the unemployed (Taylor-Gooby, 1985, p. 78). This may betoken an overt return to the ethic of the workhouse and it will, of course – at least in the short run – have implications for state expenditure on the income maintenance system. Nonetheless he questions whether this of itself constitutes a rolling back of the state from welfare. Indeed, he contends that once this and contemporary demographic factors are taken into account, the only area of welfare which the state appears to have moved out of is housing.

Sullivan (1984) similarly argues that high levels of unemployment – whether resulting from or merely accompanying Conservative government in this period – has locked the state into continued massive involvement and expenditure in systems of social security and income maintenance. Additionally, he argues that demographic factors, such as the increasing proportion of elderly people in the population, and the failure of private welfare schemes where they have been attempted (e.g. the USA), have prevented Conservative governments in the 1980s from dismantling the welfare state in health, education and the personal social services. In his view, the crisis of welfare has been deepened by new conservative policies of retrenchment but the boundaries of state involvement in welfare remain, at least for the moment, substantially intact.

O'Higgins comes to a similar conclusion:

the examination of expenditure plans under the Conservative government suggests that beliefs that it would lead to radical changes . . . are so far unfounded, not so much because the government has changed its mind, but because it has been unable to implement its rhetoric. (1983, p. 175)

The welfare state has been cut, a not insubstantial degree of restructuring and privatization has certainly occurred. But, for whatever reasons, the rhetoric of a dismantled welfare state has not yet been matched by reality. The state remains deeply enmeshed in the provision of welfare services. Certainly much more deeply enmeshed than the new conservatives would wish.

(ii) FREE MARKET AND STRONG STATE

Another paradox and one which appears to be at the heart of government policy during this period is that of the free economy and the strong state (Gamble, 1985). At one and the same time, it is argued, the Conservative governments of the early 1980s have appeared to be committed to policies to liberate the economy from state interference but also to policies which have increased the power of the state. The new conservatives have in practice, or at least so it seems, opposed state intervention at the same time as contemporary Conservative governments have become the most interventionist governments of modern times.

On the one hand, policies seem to have been directed towards rolling back the frontiers of the state in order to encourage private enterprise and voluntary exchange. Public sector enterprise and employment have been reduced, public expenditure has been reduced substantially and the number and range of public responsibilities have been limited. On the other hand, however, other policies seem to have been directed to quite different aims. The state's power and authority appear to have been strengthened by increasing funds and personnel for the security services, by weakening local control over local spending decisions, by transferring many erstwhile local government functions to central government and national bodies, and by introducing new legal controls over, for example, the activities of trade unions, political demonstrators and strikers.

In 1979, when the first government pledged to new conservative principles was elected, its programme appeared anti-state and hostile to the postwar consensus on state involvement. The surprising feature of these years is that, despite apparent moves to achieve the contraction of the state in some areas, the state appears in other areas to be more interventionist than at any other time in the modern period.

1945–85: A SUMMARY

It is commonplace to divide the forty postwar years into three periods or phases, each characterized by particular political attitudes towards state interventionism and each marked by differences in the scope of state activity. The years 1945–75 have been characterized in this chapter, as elsewhere, as thirty years of state interventions based on a postwar settlement between the political parties which established a consensus on the principles of a mixed economy and a welfare state. The short period 1975–9 has been seen as a watershed where political attitudes and state activity appeared to be those of a period of transition. Operating side by side during this period there seemed to be policies marking the high-tide mark of postwar consensus (the social contract) and the harbingers of a restricted state (monetarist economic policies).

1979–85 has been presented in some places as a period in which the postwar consensus on state involvement was well and truly broken and a new consensus – this time on a limited state – was forged. Yet, the evidence appears to suggest that, even during this period, state intervention, albeit of a different kind than hitherto, was as significant a political feature as state restriction.

Our task now, therefore, is to attempt to discern how various models of or perspectives on the state might theorize the changing nature and scope of state involvement in civil society over these four eventful postwar decades. In particular, the next chapter will attempt to present analyses which seek to explain apparent consensus and apparent contradiction over state intervention in civil society through time.

2 Perspectives on the Modern British State

The primary concern of Chapter 1 was to map out the terrain of state involvement in British society during the last forty years. Our task in this chapter is to construct a set of route maps to help us explore that terrain. We have already established the need to understand state intervention in welfare within the wider context of general state involvement in civil society. Our concern in this chapter is to explore various explanations of the pattern of state intervention which has unfolded over the last four decades. This project is developed with specific reference to state intervention in welfare in the next chapter, and an evaluation and critique of the various perspectives explored in the early chapters of this book are offered in a later chapter (Chapter 5).

In this chapter, then, we review four sets of explanatory perspectives on the British state and its involvement in social and economic life. They are

— reformist views of the state
— the state and industrial society perspective
— Marxist views of the state
— radical right views of the state

Reformist Views of the State

Here close attention is paid to the work of a number of writers, especially those associated with the Labour Party in the 1950s and 1960s, who saw themselves and became seen as the new revisionist thinkers. The work of this group of Labour intellectuals is diverse in its aims and intentions. Some of it consciously aims to provide a theory for social democracy (Crosland, 1956). Some of it was intended, when written, to inform intra-party struggles within the Labour Party between its left and right wings (Crossman, 1950; 1952; Crosland, 1952; 1956; 1974). Other work is rather more in the nature of refining or updating the original revisionist theses developed during the 1950s (e.g. Williams, 1981). Taken together, this corpus of literature allows us to construct a reformist perspective on the state and state intervention.

A Transformed State

Much of the literature on the modern British state acknowledges that the postwar settlement, based on macro-level management of a mixed economy, together with the creation and consolidation of a welfare state changed the role and functions of the British state (e.g. Crosland, 1956; Hayek, 1976; Jessop, 1980).

What is often at issue is the nature of that transformation. Each of the perspectives on the state considered in this chapter theorizes the nature of that transformation in different ways. The reformist perspective adopted by revisionist writers, arguably conceives that transformation as more fundamental than do any of the other perspectives. From this perspective, the transformation of the state in the late 1940s is seen as having been the natural concomitant of a transformation of the capitalist system itself:

> while capitalism has not collapsed as a result of internal contradictions – it is possible to see a transformation of capitalism occurring. Since 1945 capitalism has been undergoing a metamorphosis into a different system. (Crosland, in Crossman, 1952, p. 34)

Or, in Crossman's own words, 'capitalism had been civilised'.

This transformation of capitalism had occurred and was continuing for a number of reasons. Crosland (Crossman, 1952) provides the clearest account of the reasons for this capitalist transformation. First, the growth of powerful anticapitalist movements (the Labour Party, trade unions, etc.) during the early twentieth century had formed a power bloc whose aspirations for a changed society could not be ignored by Conservative or radical governments. Secondly, it is argued, the British business class coincidentally supported the political aspirations of the labour movement and therefore supported a state transformed into an interventionist state. It had done so because it benefited from state intervention policies. Full employment (one of the core prerequisites of the interventionist state) meant guaranteed high levels of consumption and production which in turn meant the generation of high profit levels. Further, it is contended that as a result of the inter-war recession the business class had lost its previously unquestioning faith in capitalism. Consequently it had developed a social conscience, having seen the social consequences of prolonged economic depression. The transformation of the state, and particularly the commitment to full employment and state welfare services, therefore occurred with the support or acquiescence of the capitalist class itself. Fourthly, the dispersion of ownership and the increasing control of industry by a managerial class had led to the transformation of capitalism. Exploitative, entrepreneurial capitalism had evolved to give birth to a system under which ownership and power had been dispersed and exploitation diminished. Finally, according to this revisionist thesis, the level of state planning developed during the Second World War had made a return to free market capitalism impossible. So, as far as the revisionist thinkers were concerned, capitalism had spawned a new economic and social system. This metamorphosis amounted to no less than the adoption by the state of the regulation of social and economic relationships in British society – a role previously occupied largely by the market.

This theme is also developed by T. H. Marshall in his work on citizenship and social class. For Marshall, the metamorphosis of capitalism was the result of a cumulative process in which new consensuses had been forged within British society over time. These related to the legal, political and social rights which citizens should enjoy in a capitalist state. With the advent of state welfare in the twentieth century a complete package of citizen rights had been integrated into the capitalist system. This package of rights regulated capitalism and protected individuals from the ravages of unbridled market forces. In so doing, capitalism had, itself, spawned a new set of economic and social institutions which had transformed its very nature (Marshall, 1963).

The Source of State Authority

Implicit in the discussion above is the view that the new, transformed and interventionist state drew its authority and legitimacy from a societal consensus which had, or so it is argued, been forged around a new conception of the relationship between state and civil society. Indeed the forging of such a consensus was itself evidence of the transformation of the capitalist system. Important elements in the creation of this new consensus included, as we have seen: the growth of a countervailing power bloc (the trade union and labour movement) and its strength relative to that of the owners of industrial capital; changes in the ownership and control structure of capitalism itself; and a realization by the representatives of industrial capital that a state which guaranteed full employment also guaranteed high profits.

We should not underestimate, however, the importance which is accorded in this perspective to the growth of social conscience as a factor in creating and moulding a new consensus. The interventionist state is seen as legitimated not only by a new accommodation to political and economic realities but also by the growth of a collective conscience. This collective conscience is seen as based on rationality and morality. It is argued that the powerful (the capitalist or business class), having witnessed at first hand the privations of the powerless (the workers, or more accurately workless) caused by prolonged economic recession, formed part of a moral and rational consensus on the need for state regulation and intervention. Such intervention would ameliorate or prevent such conditions occurring in the future. As we shall see (Chapter 3), such an analysis forms an important strand in reformist perspectives on state intervention in welfare.

The source of authority and legitimation for increased state activity in the postwar years is seen then as having been rooted in a ground swell of interest and opinion hostile to, or at least critical of, the results of unrestricted capitalism. Continued legitimation of state activity would depend on a continued social consensus in favour of intervention, but the revisionists had little doubt that consensus of opinion, if not totally irreversible, was virtually so.

The State and Government

As we shall see, the relationship between the state and government is, particularly in Marxist perspectives, theoretically problematic. For the revisionists no such problematic arises. The state, or the apparatus of government, is seen as subordinate to the will of democratically elected governments. The policies and actions of the state are no more and no less than the policies of elected governments. The policies and actions of governments are, themselves, simply responses to a societal consensus (however forged) on what government policies and actions should be. Illustrations of this approach litter the literature of social democracy but it is nowhere more clearly stated than in an essay by Strachey in Crossman's collection of Fabian essays published in the early 1950s. Commenting on what he obviously regarded as the formation of a socialist consensus in Britain in the late 1940s, Strachey argues in one and the same breath for two revisionist propositions: that the state is subordinate to government and that capitalism has been transformed by state interventionist measures. 'Keynesian fiscal measures supplemented by physical controls gave the state all the tools that were needed to enable it to do what it wanted' (Strachey, in Crossman, 1952, p. 188).

For Strachey there is no question that the state machinery was subordinate to the will of government. A new societal consensus, expressed through government policies, had meant that the early postwar period was characterized by 'governments accepting as state responsibility what had previously been left to the free market' (Crosland, 1956, p. 11). According to reformist theories, the state, though autonomous from the owners of capital, possessed no autonomy in relation to government. It was its handmaiden – no more, no less. Such a view had been very clearly expressed by Labour's first postwar Prime Minister, reflecting on the relationship between government and civil service 'that's the civil service tradition, a great tradition. They carry out the policy of any given government' (Williams, 1969, p. 79).

For the revisionists, then, the transformed state, operating within the context of a transformed capitalism, occupied a handmaiden role to government. That state, at the specific historical conjuncture of the mid-twentieth century, had been used by governments reflecting the will of the people, to encourage and legitimize the transformation of dominant values in British society from the values of competitive capitalism to values of co-operation and collectivism (Tawney, 1964, p. 169).

The Role and Functions of the State

Already it has been argued that from the reformist view the state occupies a subservient role to that of government and functions simply to implement government policy. In particular the state, as the instrument of government, functions to regulate and iron out peripheral problems in a more or less harmonious and humane social system. It also functions to lay down the ground rules which would ensure the consolidation and development of the reformist consensus which had emerged in the postwar period. Specifically the functions of the British state are, in this reformist formulation, threefold:

(1) The state acts to correct, supplement and, if necessary, supplant the market system to promote the development of greater equality, democracy and welfare in British society (George and Wilding, 1985).

It was, after all, clear to the reformists that in a liberal-democratic, mixed economy society with a plurality of power bases and economic control the state would sometimes have to operate to lay down the detailed ground rules and compel the private (and nationalized) firm to conform to its own positive views of where the public interest lies (Crosland, 1974).

> or to guide the private (and public) sector to forms of collective action to achieve collective goals which individuals cannot achieve, or cannot achieve with the same measure of success, by their isolated efforts (Crosland, 1956).

(2) The reformist state operates to modify injustices caused by a market system of resource distribution (George and Wilding, 1985).

Even in a postwar Britain characterized by the emergence of a new social consensus, the private sector of the economy was seen to be motivated by the profit motive rather than the desire to satisfy social and economic needs. The state, in such a system, would operate – largely by means of social expenditure – to redistribute resources, whether through the tax and income maintenance systems or through services in kind.

(3) The reformist state operates to develop a planned growth economy in order to facilitate redistributive social and economic policies. If the diminution of inequalities was an important goal for the revisionist socialists then it was seen as imperative that the state should act as a planning agency operating to develop Britain into a continuous growth economy generating wealth to be used for redistributive purposes.

For the revisionists then the state has clear functions to perform. Those functions are underwritten by government and rooted in a social consensus on the goals of state action. In order to perform those functions and achieve consensual goals the state would therefore act, particularly through Keynesian economic measures (Schott, in Held *et al.*, 1983), to stimulate and guide the economy, and through social welfare measures to ensure continued consensus.

In other words, according to this perspective, the state is and should be used as an agency of economic planning, regulation and reorganization to maintain full employment in the British economy. Full employment it is argued generates high production levels and additional national wealth. These, in turn, generate higher levels of social expenditure as well as facilitating higher levels of consumption.

The state, in this perspective, also acts through a strategy of increased social expenditure to ameliorate residual relative deprivation and to redistribute resources. It should be stressed here that this perspective does not promote, neither does it prescribe the eradication of inequality as one of the state's functions. Rather it sees the state functioning to modify the scope of inequalities between individuals. The provision of a welfare minimum is seen, in this perspective, as having two related aims. The first is to ameliorate and modify resource inequalities but the second, and arguably more important, is to guarantee an equality of status – rather than outcome – to all citizens through access to state welfare services (Crosland, 1956; Marshall, 1963).

Understanding State Activity in Postwar Britain

How, then, does this perspective on the state help us to understand the patterns of state involvement in the economic and social life of Britain in the postwar years?

As we have seen, large scale intervention in both economy and welfare during the three decades of interventionism is easily explained by the reformists. A new social consensus had been forged during the war and postwar years around a growth economy consisting of public and private sectors. That full employment growth economy was achieved largely as a result of state interventionist Keynesian policies of planning, stimulation and industrial reorganization. The postwar consensus also embraced the idea of using economic growth and national prosperity to enhance social expenditure and provide increased citizen access to welfare services. During this period the state, as a tool of government, which was itself responding to a wider social consensus, was an increasingly interventionist state. Its activities were marked by expansion and continuity whichever political party constituted the government. So far so good, but how does this reformist view of state and society explain state activities in the 1970s and 1980s?

Any attempt to construct a reformist perspective of state activities and the relationship between state and society during the 1970s and 1980s – and especially since 1975 – has to take account of the following empirical realities of the period:

(1) continued state interventionism, along traditional lines during the early 1970s in a period when unemployment was rising and Keynesian economic strategies seemed less successful than in earlier periods;

(2) the contradictory nature of state activity during the period 1975–9 when state incorporation of important elements of civil society was accompanied by restrictions on social expenditure;

(3) the apparent contradictions of the years following 1979 when, despite the rhetoric of a minimalist state and the realities of cuts in social expenditure and the redirection of state activities, the relationship between the state and civil society may be argued to have changed less than predicted by commentators or politicians themselves. An understanding of state activity during this period might, therefore, be found in the following analysis.

Even in the early 1970s the postwar settlement had remained the keystone of societal consensus. Government policy on state involvement and intervention also continued to be guided by the 1945 settlement. Conventional policies on state intervention during this period were, however, subject to significant strain. Keynesian economic policies, which had worked so well for much of the postwar period, no longer generated the rates of growth necessary to sustain high levels of state intervention. Unemployment was on the increase and demand for British products and the British economy in general had been hit by world-wide economic difficulties (Sked and Cook, 1979; Marwick, 1982). Attempts to resolve this strain between consensus on state involvement on the one hand and sluggish growth on the other led the Heath government of the early 1970s to experiment with policies aimed at restraining state expenditure (Sked and Cook, 1979; Marwick, 1980). This experiment was in turn abandoned as the result of public pressure and consensus in favour of the retention of the policies of the postwar settlement.

The period 1975–9 was marked by a further escalation of economic problems in Britain and elsewhere. Keynesian economic policies were seen to have failed. The Labour government of the period found itself at the centre of a set of political contradictions. On the one hand one of the cornerstones of high levels of state intervention – continued economic growth – had evaporated and pressure had been exerted on the British government by the IMF (1976) to adopt economic policies which implied extensive cuts in public spending (see Riddell, 1983). At the same time the government remained committed to reflecting in its policies the societal consensus it had helped create in the early postwar period. The result was a curious hybrid. On the one hand, in response to domestic economic conditions and external pressure, government adopted policy stances which restricted state activity in civil society (Cawson, 1982). On the other hand it appeared to develop a strategy intended both to minimize the extent to which state activity in civil society would be affected and to also elicit the consent of the British people to such a strategy. The social contract and allied policies therefore marked, for the revisionists at least, further evidence of the relationship between society, government and state described earlier. The dampening down of wage demands explicit in the social contract would help minimize cuts in social expenditure and state activity. At the same time the unpalatable economic policies adopted would be the result of a societal consensus echoing the spirit if not the aspirations of 1945. Such a consensus was to be built by the incorporation of trade unions and industrial management into the machinery of the state (Cawson, 1982).

So far, so good. But how does such a reformist perspective seek to explain the contradictions of the period since 1979? Throughout the late 1970s, the Conservative Party under their leader Margaret Thatcher had developed a set of policies and principles which we have labelled elsewhere as the new conservatism. New conservatism, as we have seen, developed a set of political principles apparently based on the ideas of individual autonomy and a minimalist state.

Reformist views would need to explain the election of new conservative Thatcher governments in 1979 and 1983 as part of a process during which there has been an attempt to forge an alternative political consensus to that represented by the 1945 settlement. Government policies and actions which have limited or changed the nature of state involvement in the economy, industry, law and order, and even housing and education might therefore be seen as drawing on a new societal consensus on social values and state activity. The restriction of the state in some areas and its greater intervention in others to ensure conformity to discipline and free market policies may in fact both resonate with and help mould contemporary public opinion.

However, elements of the old societal consensus appear also to have remained as important elements in public opinion. As Taylor-Gooby's work has shown, public consciousness appears to include commitment to both decreased and increased state activity. While many of the political, economic and social values espoused by the new conservatives may reflect the contemporary views of the British public, that same British public appears to remain committed to continued and increased state intervention, in welfare at least, as part of a package of citizen rights (Taylor-Gooby, 1985).

This reality, together with other factors such as the evidence of the outcome of new right policies in other societies (see p. 26), can be seen by the holders of a reformist perspective to support their view of the relationship between society, government and state. Specifically it can be used to argue that

(1) the restriction and reorientation of state activity in the 1980s is a response by government to a newly forged social consensus,
   but
(2) that the new consensus is not, at this point, without its own contradictions for it retains, at least for the time being, elements of the old consensus which restricts government's freedom to further roll back the state.

The State and Industrial Society Perspective

In this section the views of a number of writers are considered as constituting a perspective on the state which regards state action to regulate social and economic relationship, or to bring about social change, as intimately bound up with what is argued to be the core prerequisite of all industrial societies – namely the development of industry and technology. Like the reformist perspective it has its roots in a functionalist sociological approach. Its emphasis is, however, quite different. Reformists see the state as acting to create or facilitate consensus and social cohesion around a set of values and opinions. According to the industrial state perspective the state acts to mould the social structure of industrial societies around the prerequisite of industrial development (Kerr, 1962; Dunning and Hopper, 1966).

This approach had considerable influence in social adminis-tration, especially during the early 1960s. A detailed account of the implications of this approach for understanding welfare appears in Chapter 3. In this chapter we elucidate the model which this approach constructs of state, government and society.

A Transformed State

Like reformist perspectives, this approach presents the idea of a transformation of the state as the key to understanding recent and contemporary activities or interventions in civil society. In this perspective, however, the crucial transformation is argued to have occurred much earlier – at the time of the Industrial Revolution – and to have been rooted in a societal transform-ation from an agrarian economic base to an industrial economic base (Galbraith, 1972). It is true, of course, that some of the proponents of this approach concede further transformations of the state at later dates. Galbraith, like the revisionist writers, sees the state as having undergone a further transformation in the twentieth century, but for him this later transformation was from the state as the executive committee of capitalist enterprise to the organizing committee of corporatism in an industrial society (1972, p. 298). From the reformist perspective, state activities in modern society are best understood if we understand them as 'civilising of capitalism' (Crossman, 1952). From the present viewpoint, state activities are, as we shall see, best understood if we understand the process of industrialization.

The Source of State Authority

The modern state, especially in its interventionist activities in civil society, draws its authority and its legitimation from what is sometimes termed the logic of industrialism (Kerr *et al.*, 1962, p. 33). Kerr and his collaborators, and indeed other writers in this area (Dunning and Hopper, 1966), see a functional relationship between industrial technology and the social structure of industrialized societies. Indeed, it is argued, the social structure of society responds to imperatives intrinsic to the industrializing process. For technological determinists there is, then, an inevitability about social structural responses. The logic of industrialism as it were pulls the social structure into line with the requirements of industrial development. So that, if the industrial system requires regulation of demand for its products together with an educated and healthy workforce, then the social structure will respond by establishing demand mechanisms and well-organized education and health services. The motor of industrial society is the industrializing process. The logic of industrialism can, therefore, be seen as providing the authority and legitimation for the state which acts, in response to that logic, to regulate or change elements of the social structure of society. It does so by establishing the mechanisms by which industrialism is serviced (economic and social policies) (Galbraith, 1972).

The State and Government

From this perspective, as from reformist views, the state is seen as merely the instrument or machinery of government. The state is subservient to government but government is in turn subservient to the logic of industrialism. State activities are,

therefore, in the last analysis predetermined by technological
and industrial development.

The Role and Functions of the State

As will already be obvious, the state is seen as occupying a
handmaiden role to the process of industrialization and
industrial development. It is no more than the instrument of
the industrial system. We must be careful, however, to
distinguish between this relationship between the state and the
industrial *system* and the relationship of the state to industrial
corporations. The state responds inevitably to the interests of the
former but it may well function against the perceived interests
of individual corporations when those interests do not correlate
with the long term interests of the industrial system as a whole.
So, for example, individual corporations may oppose, at
particular historical conjunctures, social expenditure on, say,
public health and education provision. However, the state may
well respond by holding such expenditure constant, or by
increasing it. From this perspective the state would then be
seen as acting in the long term interests of the industrial
system, which needs a constant supply of educated, healthy
workers, albeit that such state activities run counter to the
perceived short term interests of individual corporations.
Indeed, although the state is seen as the handmaiden of the
industrial system, that role does not preclude quite extensive
state activities. Given the complex nature of industrial technology and the tensions between the system and its component
parts, on the one hand, and the complexities of distribution of
the products of industry, on the other, the state becomes the
key regulatory agency in civil society as well as an agency
providing support services for the industrial system (Kerr *et al.*,
1962; Mishra, 1981).

The state may therefore function at particular historical
points to plan, control or regulate economic development, its
activities depending on the specific needs of the industrial
system at any one particular time (Galbraith, 1972). It may act
to reorganize or reorient industrial development when such
changes foster the interests of the industrial system as a whole,

as with state actions that accompanied rapid technological development in Britain in the 1960s. At times the state may intervene in civil society to provide large scale state welfare services to facilitate industrial development. At other times industrial development may, itself, demand changed or less extensive support services and the state therefore, responds accordingly.

So, the industrial state responds to the demands of the industrial system as the motor vehicle responds to the demands of its driver. At times its activities are unhampered by the brake and it speeds away. At other times circumstances demand that its activities are restrained or redirected. Our concern, therefore, in the next section of this chapter is to demonstrate how such a model of state and society explains state activities in Britain in the postwar period.

Understanding State Activity in Postwar Britain

This approach like other modernization theories, and indeed like the erstwhile popular 'end of ideology' thesis (Bell, 1960), presents an understanding of state involvement in society rooted in the idea that societal development is inevitably dependent to a far greater extent on material forces in society than it is on the resolution of conflicting ideologies.

It is simple enough to see how this perspective explains increased state intervention in postwar British society and the almost continuous growth of state activities during the extended postwar boom. The rapid industrial development of the early postwar years demanded that the state respond through the use of macroeconomic demand management to ensure markets for increased industrial production. The growth of the industrial system in this period also demanded a measure of central planning. The need for technological development of industry in the 1960s similarly demanded state intervention in economy and industry to reorganize the industrial base (Galbraith, 1972).

Throughout the period, industrial development also called forth the inevitable involvement of the state in welfare provision. State activity in education and health was essential in order to provide appropriately skilled and healthy workers. It was necessary in personal social services to provide support services for geographically (and socially) mobile workers and their families, bereft of traditional support networks – including the extended family – by the demands of industrial development. It was necessary in housing so that workers and their families could be housed in the areas of their new work places.

It is also possible to see how such an approach might seek to explain part of the pattern of state activities in Britain since the early 1970s. As unemployment increases, and new technological developments seem to herald a possibly permanent end to the need for full employment, then cuts in welfare expenditure might be seen as inevitable and necessary concomitants to changes in the industrial system. It might even be possible to extend the boundaries of this approach in order to explain certain reorientations in state policy and expenditure during the late 1970s and early 1980s. Law and order policies may be viewed as reflecting changes in the industrial system. A depressed (or recessed) industrial system might be seen as presenting problems of social control as poverty and disappointed expectations of full employment may lead to increased criminal activity, itself necessitating increased law enforcement resources rather than increased welfare developments.

What is more difficult to see is how such an approach might explain a series of apparent contradictions in state activity during this period. Why, for instance, should industrial and economic recession be accompanied in the mid 1970s by increased levels of state planning and ownership of industry (witness the introduction of legislation and state planning and ownership agencies such as the National Enterprise Board) but, in the early 1980s, by an apparent large scale withdrawal from central planning and state ownership of industry? Why should deepening industrial and economic problems in the late 1970s apparently have elicited from the state a political strategy of corporatism and incorporation, while economic crisis in the early 1980s has been accompanied by a rejection of such strategies?

Detailed consideration of these problems can be found in a

later chapter (Chapter 5) but, even at this point, these problems might appear to discredit, to a greater or lesser extent, the industrial state approach as an underarching explanation of state activity in modern Britain.

Marxist Views of the State

More extensive, detailed and sophisticated summaries of Marxist theories of the state exist than the one which follows (Gold, Lo and Wright, 1975; Jessop, 1977). Readers will also find in the now quite extensive corpus of work on the state in capitalist society (Miliband, 1969; 1982; Poulantzas, 1972; 1975; Jessop, 1977; 1980) much richer accounts of the diverse analyses, controversies and debates within Marxist scholarship about the nature, role and functions of the capitalist state. Our concern here is to present systematically those contributions from Marxist scholarship which might begin to help us make sense of the development of state social and economic intervention in modern Britain.

An ambiguity or duality about the nature of the state in capitalist society appears to exist in the writings of Marx himself. On the one hand, he appears to argue that the state is no more and no less than the organizing committee of a ruling or capitalist class which acts, at all times, to promote, foster and protect the economic cultural and ideological interests of that class (Marx, 1967). However, in other places he appears to argue that the state has a degree of autonomy from society in general and from a ruling class or elite in particular. In the *18th Brumaire*, for example, he appears to suggest that the state does not merely co-ordinate society in the interests of a ruling class. Rather it can in particular circumstances – especially when there is a relative balance of social class forces – promote changes and developments in civil society which are not immediately recognizable as actions in the interest of a dominant class (Marx, 1973). What follows, therefore, is an attempt to describe how this duality is reflected in Marxist writing on the state. We therefore trace two approaches –

which may be described as system determinist (or Marxist functionalist) and relative autonomy approaches – to see what they have to say about the activities and nature of the state in society.

A Transformed State

We have seen that both reformist and industrial state views present the idea of a transformed state as an aid to understanding state activity in modern Britain. Marxist theories of the state also depend, in part, on the idea of state transformation. For some writers transformations or changes in the activities of the state simply reflect accommodations to changes in the nature of capitalism over time. They amount to little more than historically specific strategies to promote the interests of a dominant class. Thus, if the state in twentieth-century capitalist countries intervenes in the economy to stabilize demand for industrial products in a way hitherto unknown, there is a straightforward explanation for such activity. Entrepreneurial capitalism has been replaced during the present century by corporate capitalism, and the greater complexity of corporate capitalism and its greater distance from the market for its products demand state intervention (Mandel, 1968; Baran and Sweezy, 1968).

Similarly, if the state in modern times has intervened in welfare to a far greater extent than hitherto, then such intervention, and the transformation of state activities which it betokens, are again merely historically specific strategies to protect the interests of a capitalist class. Welfare interventions may have been introduced further to ensure stability of consumption for corporate capitalism (Mandel, 1968), to provide an appropriately socialized, educated and healthy workforce for capitalist enterprise (Saville, 1957; O'Connor, 1973), or to supplement the repressive and ideological state apparatuses with a conformative element (Barratt-Brown, 1972). State transformations are, then, from a system determinist Marxist approach more illusory than real.

Other Marxist writers, however, accord greater significance to transformations in state activity. Jessop, commenting on the fundamental changes in state activity in the early postwar period, is in little doubt that 'this produced a major transformation of the British state and also implied a fundamental social democratisation of the political system' (Scase, 1980, p. 27). Policy interventions by the state during this century are similarly seen by other writers as reflecting real rather than illusory transformations in the relationship between state, society and social classes, whether temporary or permanent. For some, such transformations reflect a limited autonomy for the state from a ruling class (Miliband, 1969), for others they reflect a much greater degree of autonomy through which the interests of all members of society are expressed through the workings of the capitalist state (Offe and Ronge, 1975).

As we shall see in a later section, these differences in emphasis imply quite different analyses of the role and functions of the capitalist state as well as of the sources of its legitimacy.

The Source of State Authority

Whereas the reformist perspective sees society as characterized by a broad social consensus on values, goals and interests, of which state action is merely a reflection, Marxist theories of the state are rooted in analyses which see society as characterized by value, goal and interest conflict. Such conflicts are seen as rooted in the fundamental conflict between a dominant or ruling class and a subordinate or working class. However, this conflict view of society yields somewhat different analyses of the sources of state authority from the system determinists on the one hand and the relative autonomists on the other.

Put simply, a system determinist view sees the ultimate authority for state intervention in civil society as being the interests of a dominant social class. That class may seek through some, or all, of those state actions to legitimize its interests by presenting class interests as national or universal interests (George and Wilding, 1976; 1985) but the final authority for state action lies in promoting ruling class interests, whether through actions aimed at creating the conditions for optimum capital accumulation or through interventions aimed at legitimizing that process (O'Connor, 1973).

Put equally simply, relative autonomy approaches permit the interpretation that the authority and legitimacy of the state (and of state interventions) rest in the theoretical or actual possibility of the state acting in the interests of a wider constituency than that represented by a dominant social class. That autonomy may be restricted to acting, at times, against certain sections of the dominant class (Poulantzas, 1973; 1975), or may be extensive enough to allow, at times, representation of apparently conflicting interests (Ginsburg, 1979; Gough, 1979). Nonetheless, for the relative autonomists the source of authority for state activity and the legitimacy of state intervention is built on a more extensive foundation than that erected by the system determinists.

The State and Government

Whereas reformist and industrial state writers perceive an unproblematic relationship between state and government and see the former as being the instrument of the latter, Marxist writers see the relationship as a problematic one. Marxists, whether from the system determinist or relative autonomy strands of thought, are united in their agreement on the following:

(1) The state is to a greater or lesser extent generally predisposed to act in the long term interests of a dominant class in society. This may be because of the social provenance of senior state personnel (instrumental theories of the state, Miliband, 1969; 1978; 1982). It may be as the result of a class structure which ensures ruling class dominance of the state whatever the social provenance of its personnel (structuralist theories of the state, Poulantzas, 1973; 1975).

(2) Such a state will therefore tend to act as a conservative force, at least for much of the time.

(3) Therefore, whatever the possibilities of state autonomy from a dominant class, for most of the time the state will

act as a conservative force whatever the political com-
plexion of government.

In general, therefore, the state will occupy a relationship to
government which is at best semi-autonomous. Certainly,
during the occupancy of reforming governments the state may
not act as the subordinate instrument of government imple-
menting policy made by government but may act as an alternative, and generally more powerful, centre of policy-making.
And, in theory, if not generally in practice, the state will manifest
a similar relative autonomy from government even when
government is itself conservative in nature. Such an analysis
leads Marxists in two different directions, however. System
determinists generally argue that, as a consequence of this
analysis, the only route to social change is one predicated on
destroying the capitalist state (Mandel, 1968). Relative autonomy writers, on the other hand, argue that such an analysis
points to the need further to transform the state by taking
control of it.

The Role and Functions of the State

The foregoing discussion will have made it patently clear to
readers that, for the system determinists at least, the state
occupies a handmaiden role to the interests of capitalism and of
a dominant, ruling class or elite. For them the state, in its
interventionist activities, acts to protect, reinforce and reproduce
the economic, social and political relationships of capitalist
society (Barratt-Brown, 1972). Most importantly, it acts
through economic intervention, to promote capital accumulation
(O'Connor, 1973) or economic efficiency (Saville, 1957). It also
functions through social intervention, the provision of welfare,
to accord citizens a modicum of social rights which may in any
event aid the accumulation process. Such interventions may be
regarded as activities intended to legitimize the relationships of
capitalist society (O'Connor, 1973) or, in other analyses, as
conformative activities (Barratt-Brown, 1972). As a result,
welfare and similar state institutions and activities have been
regarded as ideological state apparatuses (Althusser, 1971).

Sociology and Social Welfare

From this viewpoint the state may also function coercively, especially during periods when the state's legitimizing or conformative activities have failed to ensure adequate levels of conformity to the values and relationships of capitalism. It may do so to ensure social stability – one of capitalism's prime requisites (Saville, 1957). This function involves, naturally enough, the legal, law enforcement and security services of the state, Althusser's repressive state apparatuses (Althusser, 1971). From this standpoint, then, the state

by its very nature . . . is simply coercive power used to protect the system of rights and duties of one process of economic relationships from invasion by another class which seeks to change them in the interest of another process. (Laski, 1934, p. 118)

In contrast, a somewhat different picture emerges from the work of those writers who theorize the existence of a degree of relative autonomy for the state from the interests of capitalism and a ruling class. Relative autonomy theories of the state present a wide range of views of the role and functions of the state in capitalist society.

Poulantzas (Poulantzas 1973; 1975), arguing that the capitalist class is less homogeneous than system determinist approaches allow, sees the dominant class as composed of class fractions (industrial capital, finance capital, etc.) which may, from time to time, have different and competing interests. He develops a model of the state which presents the state as relatively autonomous from each and all of these class fractions but as acting in the long term interests of capitalism. It does so by performing functions and activities which protect the long term survival interests of capitalism as a system. The state, therefore, adopts a semi-autonomous role in relation to the different sectors of the capitalist class but functions to perpetuate the capitalist class system.

Other writers see the state as predisposed to adopt a supportive role to the capitalist system but as functioning in a secondary and contingent way to promote some of the interests of subordinate social classes:

From the working class view, it is a response to their continual struggle . . . From the capitalist point of view it has contributed to the continual struggle to accumulate capital . . . in bringing labour and capital together profitably. (Ginsburg, 1979, p. 2)

Still others (Gough, 1979, for instance) see the state's relative autonomy as manifest especially during periods of approximate balance in the social class struggle. At such times the state may function to promote interests which are not those of a dominant class and its role may therefore be seen as one of representing majority interests in society (Offe and Ronge, 1975).

Yet another strand in this relative autonomy thesis points up state activities which appear to reflect a coincidental coalition of interests between social classes at particular times. Such a strand, therefore, comes near to presenting the state as capable, at particular historical points, of reflecting and moulding a national or supra-class interest (see Bellaby, 1977, for instance).

The role and functions of the state in capitalist society are, then, seen from a somewhat different perspective by system determinists, on the one hand, and relative autonomy writers on the other. Such differences stem from different conceptions of the relationship between the state and social class(es) and are also reflected in different ways in which they seek to explain state intervention in British society in the postwar period.

Understanding State Activity in Postwar Britain

Marxist explanations of state activity in postwar Britain provide a rich, complex and diverse set of accounts of the reasons for state interventionism (Saville, 1957; Mandel, 1968; Baran and Sweezy, 1968; Offe and Ronge, 1975; Gough, 1979; Offe, 1984). While system determinist writers tend to perceive state interventionist policies as performing functional tasks aimed at perpetuating a capitalist system of social organization, other Marxist writers concede the existence of a less deterministic relationship between state activity and capitalist interests.

For the system determinists there is an almost inevitable relationship between the interests of a capitalist class and the activities of the state. Thus the Keynesian economic strategy of demand management adopted in the early postwar years may be seen as little more than state activity designed to promote the interests of the owners of capital in British society (Baran and Sweezy, 1968). Planned full employment in a controlled economy stimulated demand and consumption and contributed to a process of capital accumulation. Or, in a slightly weaker variant of the system determinist line, intervention in economy and industry – whilst a concession to an ascendant subject class – was planned and implemented in such a way that the economic interests of a capitalist class would not be damaged and may indeed have been improved (Schott, 1982).

The large scale intervention of the state in welfare through the creation and consolidation of a welfare state may, from this approach, also be seen as part of a strategy of state activities aimed at protecting and promoting the interests of capital. So that the creation of a national health service might be seen as promoting the economic interests of capitalism by maintaining the health of workers and potential workers. Education provision might be seen as promoting both economic and ideological interests by functioning to produce appropriately skilled and appropriately socialized workers, and so on (see Chapter 3 for a further treatment of these issues).

State intervention to reorganize or reorient industry in the 1960s, together with specific welfare interventions in education and income maintenance, can be seen, through the eyes of the system determinists, as providing further evidence that state intervention in civil society functions to protect, promote and reinforce capitalist interests.

The expansion of higher education with a concomitant emphasis on technology, together with the reorganization of secondary education, took place at a time when the state was also increasing its interventionist powers in order to modernize industry and facilitate technological development. Each of these initiatives might be seen as part of an interventionist package to increase Britain's industrial competitiveness and facilitate quicker economic growth which, in turn, would contribute to increased levels of profit for the owners of capital. The introduction of a new element in the income maintenance system, namely an earnings related unemployment benefit offering reasonably high levels of benefit to the frictionally unemployed, might be seen as a welfare intervention aimed at minimizing the opposition of labour organizations to such economic and industrial restructuring.

The picture that emerges, then, is of an interventionist state functioning, at least until the end of the 1960s, in a way which, while maintaining full employment and providing extensive welfare services, ultimately served the interests of a dominant social class. The pattern of state intervention in the 1970s and 1980s can be theorized in the following way.

During the earliest postwar period the process of capital accumulation had been aided by the activities of an interventionist state operating a demand management economic strategy. Economic planning, a strategy of full employment and welfare interventions had together formed the basis for economic growth and the protection of the economic interests of a dominant class. However, by the early 1970s Keynesianism was in crisis. The British economy – whose growth had, in any case, been slower than planned, or that of its competitors – was faltering. Unemployment was rising. In such a situation, a comprehensive system of welfare services and high levels of public spending which had, hitherto, complemented capital accumulation now had the opposite effect. High levels of public expenditure, taking up an ever increasing proportion of gross national product, threatened capital accumulation rather than aiding it (O'Connor, 1973). In these new circumstances, this new contradiction of capitalism – as it was seen – was best resolved by state activity aimed at reducing public expenditure, and therefore state intervention in some areas. This was particularly so in those areas appropriately resourced in a growth economy – for example, education and health – but inappropriate to the needs of a contracting economy with a slack labour market. Important elements of state interventionist powers, especially in economic and industrial planning and control, were retained by governments anticipating the deepening recession to be but part of a cyclical process of slump and boom. Most notably, both sides of industry were incorporated, at least partially, into the machinery of the state in an attempt to manage the recession by consent.

With the deepening of economic crisis in Britain in the late 1970s and early 1980s, however, came new patterns of state activity aimed at shoring up and, if possible, improving the prospects of the owners of capital. The state, acting as the 'politically conscious directorate' of capital and aided by a new Conservative government substantially shorn of adherence to the aristocratic paternalism of previous Conservative governments, set about steering a new course. The contradictory nature of state involvement in the 1970s had failed to halt economic decline. Public spending restrictions co-ordinated by a corporate state had failed woefully to staunch Britain's economic wounds. Capitalism and state involvement was therefore to move into a new stage with new guiding principles. They were to be

(1) a rolling back of the state from large scale expenditure and involvement in the public sector of industry and the public services (including welfare). This dismantling of the interventionist state would allow market forces to reassert themselves as the guiding hand of the economy. Such a free market, released from the burden of financing public enterprises and services, would reverse Britain's economic fortunes and lead to a growth in profitability.

(2) a specific intention to dismantle the welfare state: its support functions were, after all, unnecessary in a possibly permanent period of high unemployment. Individual, family and community 'needs' for welfare should be met, wherever possible by individuals, families and communities. The legitimation of dominant values previously facilitated by elements of the Welfare State (e.g. education and personal social services) would, less expensively, be achieved by coercive means.

(3) the removal of controls on the export of capital, which would facilitate capital accumulation by permitting investment in high profit economies such as those in the Far East.

As we have seen in Chapter 1, such a strategy for state activity in the 1980s has thrown up a number of paradoxes or contradictions. That the rhetoric and reality of rolling back the state do not completely match each other is indisputable. High levels of unemployment have meant increased public spending on income maintenance provisions. The failure of insurance schemes for health and education in other societies has, perhaps, inhibited the privatization of welfare services, though it has not prevented restrictions in spending. It may even be that public resistance has obstructed a more rapid and substantial removal of the state from the arena of civil society. Marxists who adopt a system determinist approach must, however, conceptualize such difficulties as pointing up the contradictions capitalism has created for itself rather than as in any part reflecting a political struggle not yet resolved. The state is experiencing temporary difficulties in removing itself from crucial areas of social and economic life. Those difficulties are accompanied, as we have seen, by a need to strengthen the state in some other areas. Such contradictions, however, demonstrate contemporary problems in representing the interests of a social class of which the state is a creature. They do not and cannot illustrate that the British state in the 1980s, as in other periods, is caught in a tension between two sets of conflicting interests, neither of which it fully represents.

Those writing from a less determinist Marxist position appear to understand state activity in the postwar period somewhat differently. From the standpoint of some (Miliband, 1969; 1978; 1982) the state has, during this period, seldom acted to promote the interests of sections of the population other than a dominant elite or class. This is largely so because of the similarity in social provenance and social values between that dominant elite and senior state functionaries. Nonetheless the state is seen, at least theoretically, as an arena of struggle capable of transformation by means of the replacement of its functionaries and, consequently, their interests and values.

Others see certain interventions by the state, during the period, as having actually reflected the interests of a much wider constituency than a small elite. The creation and early consolidation of the welfare state may be seen as an example of such interventions reflecting the state's relative autonomy and capacity to act on behalf of wider interests, especially at times in which the balance of power between social classes in society is more evenly poised than at others (Gough, 1979). Some proponents of this approach would also wish to explain some interventionist developments as truly reflecting the dialectical nature of class struggle; so that the reorganization of secondary education (Bellaby, 1977) and the expansion of higher education, to take but two examples, may be seen as activities yielding advantages to competing social class interests while failing to satisfy the total demands of either. Thus the provision of secondary and higher education, ostensibly aimed at producing equality of opportunity to students from different social classes, may be seen as partially reflecting that aspiration as well as producing appropriately educated and socialized person power for capitalist enterprise.

The ultimate failure of Keynesianism in the 1970s and the overload of government (O'Connor, 1973) threw organized labour on to the defensive and, in such circumstances, the state more clearly acted in the interests of a ruling elite. Nonetheless, the failure of the Thatcher governments to fully implement policies of state retrenchment should be seen in part as a response to growing resistance to such retrenchment from wider sections of the population (Taylor-Gooby, 1985).

Radical Right Views on the State

Even the most cursory of reading of the 'giants' of the radical right (Hayek, 1944; 1949; 1960; 1973; 1979; Friedman, 1962; 1980), or, indeed, of their contemporary British disciples (Seldon, 1967; 1981; Powell, 1969; Boyson, 1971; Joseph and Sumption, 1979; Harris and Seldon, 1979) leaves the reader in no doubt that, for the writers and actors of the radical right, extensive state activity in civil society is to be regretted. It has, during the last forty years, translated aspirations into citizen rights (Powell, 1972, p. 12). It has overturned a free market system which acted as a guarantor of individual freedom. The interventionist state has substantially transformed an earlier form of social organization in which political power was held by one group and economic power by a countervailing force which could use its power to block state coercion (Friedman, 1962). It has created business and labour monopolies which limit voluntary exchange. It has fostered waste and inefficiency and reduced the population to the status of serfdom (Hayek, 1944).

For the radical right, analysis of the state and prescription of its activities are a straightforward process.

A Transformed State

Radical right commentators are quite clear that the increased involvement of the state in the affairs of civil society since 1945 mark a transformation in the nature of the state. That transformation is perceived as having been from a minimalist state with residual economic and social functions to a collectivist state with extensive central planning functions in the economy and welfare (Hayek, 1960). More sharply, the transformation is seen by some as having replaced a liberal non-interventionist state with an embryonic socialist state conducive to the development of an authoritarian society (e.g. Powell, 1969).

The Source of State Authority

As we have seen already, different perspectives on the state offer quite different analyses of the processes which legitimize interventionist state activity. From the reformist viewpoint, the source of state authority is seen as being rooted in a societal consensus on the need for an interventionist state which functions to transform, or humanize, the capitalist system. For the industrial state writers, the logic of industrialism provides the key to understanding state activity and the source of authority for it. For Marxists writing from a system determinist standpoint, the logic of capitalism – and particularly of capital accumulation – acts as the source of legitimation for state activity. For the relative autonomy writers, state activities are

legitimated because the state is an arena of struggle, theoretically, and sometimes actually, capable of representing the
interests of a wider constituency than a ruling class or elite.

For writers from the radical right none of these understandings will suffice. Rather the state, in its interventionist
activities, has drawn support from a social consensus created
through a process of misapprehension. For these writers the
interventionist state is a half-way house to socialism or, indeed,
'socialism by stealth' (Powell, 1969). The British population
has been misled by well-meaning but mistaken men (sic) who
have drawn the British public and state along the road to
collectivism and will, if unimpeded, create an authoritarian
state and a subject, fettered people (Hayek, 1944; Friedman,
1980). Put quite simply, the state's authority for interventionist
actions is bogus, is rooted in the creation of a false consensus
based on false premisses and is the subject of close scrutiny.

The State and Government

Radical right views of the relationship between state and
government are very interesting. It will be clear by now that
the ultimate aim of the radical right thinkers is the creation of a
society in which the state undertakes minimal functions and
intervenes in civil society only in those few areas where market
regulation and provision is inappropriate or inefficient (Boyson,
1971; Harris and Seldon, 1979; Seldon, 1981). Radical right
views on what would constitute authority to roll back the state
provide us with an interesting insight into how the relationship
between government and state is theorized. It has been a central
argument of proponents of this view on the state that the sole
authority for a minimalist state would be that gained through
an electoral mandate and, as we have seen, the source of
authority for postwar state interventionism is argued to have
been a societal consensus, albeit based on a form of false
consciousness (Powell, 1972). What emerges, therefore, is a
view that the level of state activity in society has been and can
be regulated by the political will of societal members. That
political will, however formed, is reflected in support for a
particular political party as party of government and that

government once so elected occupies a superordinate position to the state. The writers of the new right, in this respect at least, have a notion of the state which is surprisingly close to that of the reformist writers.

The Role and Functions of the State

For much of the postwar period the state has, from this perspective, played a role which, despite the legitimacy ascribed by a societal consensus, promoted the interests of collectivism and collective planning and demoted the interests of individual freedom and democracy. Specifically the state, as a result of its interventionist activities, has functioned in such a way that the fabric of a civilized society and healthy economy have been threatened.

For the anti-collectivist writers of the new right, collectivist or interventionist state activities have been socially disruptive, have reduced freedom, have wasted resources and have promoted economic inefficiency (George and Wilding, 1976; 1985). State interventionism, particularly in welfare, has raised expectations, through a theory of universal services, that individual *needs* should be treated as individual *rights*. It has disappointed those expectations for a variety of reasons – detailed in the next chapter – and has therefore acted as a disruptive force in British society. State provision of services in many areas has created virtual monopolies, with the resultant effects of leaving limited individual freedom of choice in the consumption of services (Powell, 1972) and of wasting resources because of the removal of competition which would have encouraged careful stewardship of resources.

In contrast to this, the theorists of the radical right have argued, the state should be substantially withdrawn from essentially political activities. It should perform only residual economic/social functions in a society reformed to permit maximum individual freedom and minimum state interference. In such a society economic efficiency and growth as well as individual choice would be promoted by the mechanisms of a free market. The state's functions would be limited to those areas which 'cannot be handled through the market at all, or can be handled at so great a cost that the use of political channels may be preferable' (Friedman, 1962, p. 25). Such functions would be:

a rule making and arbitration function and in particular the administration of legal and justice systems;

a function to provide services where state monopoly is likely to be more technically efficient than competitive non-state provision (perhaps rail services and the like);

and

a function to provide services and design policies for individuals no longer capable of making informed individual choices (such as the mentally ill and the mentally handicapped). (George and Wilding, 1976)

Such an understanding of state functions in the past and such prescriptions for state activities in the future are, of course, reflected in the following discussion of the postwar British state.

Understanding State Activity in Postwar Britain

Here, as elsewhere in the writings of the new right, explanations are deceivingly simple. If we are to understand the large scale interventionist activities of the state during the three decades of interventionism we only have to understand one thing. Successive governments, as well as generations of British people, fell prey to the 'false trails of Butskellism', to a vision of planned economy (albeit a mixed economy), full employment and rights to welfare. They were misled, and misled themselves, into believing that central state intervention could create a just, humane and efficient society. In so doing governments, as well as people, while rejecting the ends of authoritarian socialism, embraced the means of achieving those ends.

That such a process should be reversed, or at least inhibited from the mid 1970s on, was the result of a number of factors.

Chief among them, however, were the following:

(1) A failure by the interventionist state to achieve the aims set for it whether of sustained economic growth or of the provision of universal, non-stigmatizing welfare services. Such failures perceived by people and governments threw seriously into question the hope that state interventionism could ever fulfil its promise.

(2) The effect of government overload. Throughout the three decades following 1945, successive governments had increased levels of state intervention in British society. By the mid 1970s it had become crystal clear that, with the failure of Keynesian economic policies to generate domestic economic growth and with the economic storm clouds gathering over the world economy, state activities of the scope already existing could no longer be financed.

Such a logic became apparent to the Labour government of the mid 1970s and led to certain limited changes in state expenditure. The new conservative governments of the early 1980s have been instrumental in attempting to consolidate a new consensus on restricted state activity and their policies reflect a commitment to further restrictions.

In this chapter, then, we have described four very different approaches or perspectives on the state. In the chapter which follows these sets of understandings are developed to provide explanations of the development and functions of the British welfare state.

3 *Approaches to Welfare*

The second chapter of this book was primarily concerned to present a range of explanations of and prescriptions for state intervention in the social and economic organization of British society. The various explanatory models considered there yielded significantly different interpretations of the nature, role and functions of the contemporary British state. In consequence, they also yielded different understandings of state activities in postwar Britain.

The aim of this chapter is to introduce, or reintroduce, the reader to a variety of perspectives – each having roots in one, or other, of the models of state and society previously considered – which seek to explain the development and functions of state involvement in the provision of social welfare. The theoretical interrelationships between particular ideas about welfare and particular sociological models of state and society will be drawn out and where appropriate the prescriptive implications for state activity in welfare contained in the approaches will be elucidated.

Specifically, the chapter comprises a description of four approaches to the development and functions of state welfare provision.

— reformist views of welfare
— the industrial state and welfare approach
— the capitalist state and welfare approach
— 'radical right' views of welfare

A body of literature has recently developed on feminism and welfare (Wilson, 1977; 1980; Loney, Boswell and Clarke, 1984; Dale and Foster, 1986). This chapter also draws on this literature and seeks to locate particular strands of feminist thought on welfare within some of the various approaches to welfare and the state.

The chapter is concerned to describe rather than to assess these various approaches (an assessment of approaches to the state, social welfare and social work can be found in Chapter 5). Nonetheless, it serves an important purpose for the student of social welfare because contained within it are descriptions of distinct approaches on the state and social welfare which may have both moulded and reflected the apparent postwar consensus on state intervention in welfare and the comparatively recent breakdown of that apparent consensus.

Reformist Views of Welfare

The views considered under this heading are drawn from the work of a collection of writers whose work has emerged over some fifty or so years. Some are social science academics, some are politicians, some are social welfare practitioners – and some are all three. Despite the differences of time and professional location which characterizes this group of authors and despite the differences in ideological and intellectual emphasis within this body of work, certain core assumptions emerge from the literature. These shared core assumptions, which have dominated the teaching of social administration and social work until comparatively recently, and arguably still strongly influence the practice of social work, have been identified in an earlier chapter but bear repeating before detailed consideration of the different variants of reformist views of welfare.

In the first place, the following views of welfare all seem to be grounded in the assumption that the state, its institutions and its functionaries are subordinate to the will of democratically elected governments. In other words, the literature in this approach assumes that the state plays no independent – or countervailing – role in the process of social policy development and the definition of policy aims and functions. The civil service and other state institutions are seen simply as adminis-

trative arms of government in the drafting and implementation
of governmental policy. Secondly there is an assumption that
governmental decisions about the scope and nature of state
intervention in social welfare reflect and are responses to wider
societal consensus on those issues – however that consensus has
been created. Finally, reformist views on welfare appear to
assume that state involvement in welfare is beneficent in its
intention and effect.

The Social Conscience Thesis

This particular explanation of the development and functions of
state welfare can be found in much of the currently used
literature on social policy and administration. It proposes that
the development of state intervention in social welfare is best
understood in terms of a cumulative growth in the collective
social conscience of the general population (and especially of
the middle and upper classes) which is reflected in organized
state action in welfare. A consensual commitment in society to
ameliorate the problems of those in need calls forth increasing
levels of organized state welfare which are not less than the
institutionalized expression of 'the obligation a person feels to
help another in distress which derives from the recognition that
they are, in some sense, members one of another' (Hall, 1952,
p. 308). This approach further proposes that the aims and
functions of state welfare are the rectification of 'diswelfares'
suffered by some members of society so that they may
experience an improved quality of life. Implicit in these aims is
a belief that welfare will function to create greater equality of
life experience in British society.

Writers who propose a social conscience explanation of
policy development and functions include many of the most
influential writers on social policy and social welfare. Their
work usually traces the growth in state welfare intervention
since the nineteenth century, although much of it, of course,
also focusses on the important developments in state welfare
since the end of the Second World War. Because of the
immense influence of this approach, in social administration
and social work teaching, until comparatively recently, it will
be considered in some detail.

SOCIAL WELFARE DEVELOPMENT

Much of the literature which adopts this approach constructs a model of cumulative, irreversible and positive development in social policies. Implicit in the model is a belief in the primacy of rationality and morality in the ordering of social affairs. The relatively low level of state involvement in welfare before this century is explained in terms of widespread ignorance about the causes and extent of social problems. The growth of institutionalized state welfare is understood as stemming from an increased awareness of social problems and an accompanying moral conviction that they should be resolved. Ultimately, the form taken by this state reflection of a collective sense of moral obligation was the creation of a welfare state by and within a benevolent, responsive and democratic state. In and before the nineteenth century, state involvement in welfare was relatively insignificant. This relative lack of involvement is argued by some to reflect an ignorance of those social facts which would surely have prompted state action had they been known. Thus, Roof – in a study of a voluntary social welfare organization – draws our attention to the extent of deprivation and poverty encountered during the mid nineteenth century by the Charity Organization Society and other charitable agencies. She appears to suggest that ameliorative action by the state, or societal presssure for such action, was substantially absent because information which documented the extent and nature of poverty was not available.

> Few had sufficient knowledge or imagination to appreciate the plight of those who lived a precarious existence on a low and uncertain weekly wage . . . No one yet knew the full extent of poverty, for the first volume of Booth's great survey was not published until 1892. (Roof, 1972, p. 24)

Similarly, Marshall (Marshall, 1975) argues that societal and governmental perceptions of late-nineteenth-century poverty were the result of ignorance. Poverty was seen as caused by individual – especially moral – deficiencies only until the agitation of the poor against intolerable social conditions and the corroborative evidence of intellectuals enlightened that ignorance.

So, the insignificance of state activity in welfare in earlier
centuries is understood in terms of general ignorance of social
problems. The growing involvement of the state in this area
during this century, which culminated in the emergence of a
welfare state is explained in similarly unproblematic terms.
Previously, social problems in British society were regarded as
insignificant in scope and generated by individual inadequacies.
The dissemination of evidence which documented the extent of
social deprivation and need, and provided interpretations of
problem causation which did not rely solely on notions of
individual pathology, resulted in a sense of social obligation,
especially among the upper and middle classes, to ameliorate
the conditions of the disadvantaged. The emergence of a new
and informed consensus is, in turn, the engine which propels
the development of state welfare policies. Social policies of the
early twentieth century are seen as the state response to this
rational and moral consensus. The enlargement of state activity
into a welfare state is seen as born out of

> an era of moral shock and remorse caused by the relation of
> the appalling conditions of the poor shown to exist by
> Charles Booth's great inquiry into the *Life and Labour of the
> People of London* and other investigations. A sense of
> compassion combined with the pangs of conscience led to a
> middle and upper class revolt against a state of affairs that
> had now become intolerable. (Robson, 1976, p. 34)

The process of social policy creation by government and
state is seen as a mysterious process but one founded on a
consensus of ideas about the need for state welfare rather than
as a process characterized by a conflict of interests between
social classes or social groups and between government and
state institutions. Quite simply

> education is provided because knowledge is believed to be
> good and ignorance a bad thing. Disease is treated because
> health is looked upon as more desirable than sickness.
> Income is maintained because poverty is regarded as an
> evil . . . (Slack, 1966, p. 40)

The development of state social policies constitutes the

institutionalization of a groundswell of social altruism. Governments and the state express the will of the people and use state power to intervene in the field of social welfare and provide a system of state financed, state controlled social services.

Before this century, state involvement in welfare had been limited to a range of activities for the relief of poverty and disease. Such activities, as we have previously noted, were grounded in an analysis of social problems which firmly located the cause of such problems in deficiencies in the victims' personalities (see, for example, George, 1973, pp. 6–12, on the philosophies implicit in poverty relief programmes).

According to the social conscience writers, early-twentieth-century state social policies on income maintenance, compulsory education and health care marked a shift in the scope and nature of state intervention to resolve social problems, and were underpinned by a changed understanding of social problem causation. Increased knowledge about the extent and context of poverty together with the political agitation of social reformers and the poor themselves were contributing factors leading to the social reforms of the 1906–11 Liberal governments (see Gregg, 1967, pp. 8–13, for a description of these reforms and the factors claimed to have influenced their enactment).

Such informed, and essentially moral, responses to the discovery of socially caused needs has, according to these writers, characterized state intervention in welfare throughout this century. The process of state provision of welfare reached its zenith during the 1940s with the enactment of a package of policies which we now regard as having been the cornerstone of the British welfare state. Beveridge's social insurance scheme – codified into legislation by the National Insurance Act (1946), the National Insurance (Industrial Injuries Act) of the same year and the National Assistance Act, 1948 – is argued to have been the inevitable response of government to a recognition that poverty was often caused by unintended interruptions of earning. The scheme provided for a basic minimum income during periods of earnings interruption and is said to have contributed to the defeat of material need (see Rodgers, 1969, vol.2, chs 11 and 12). Further improvements to the scheme, such as the introduction of an earnings related unemployment benefit in the late 1960s are seen as responses to a consensual recognition that the transition from employment to unemployment, or from one job or skill to another, is often outside the control of the individual worker and should not be marked by the experience of material poverty.

Similarly, the health care plans of the wartime coalition government, and Bevan's National Health Service Act, which established the National Health Service in 1948, can be seen as the reaction of government and state to the generally recognized need for a universal health care system which should be free at the point of need for all British people. Once the full extent of the health care needs of the population had been established, no government could have acted otherwise, even if that meant tackling the problem of the relationship of the medical profession to the state (see, for example, Rodgers, 1969, vol.2, p. 50, or Brown, 1976, p. 48).

The 1944 Education Act, which ensured compulsory secondary education for all, and the introduction of comprehensive secondary education in 1965 can both be seen from a social conscience perspective as the institutionalization by state and government of the principle of equality of opportunity which had taken root in the minds of the British people. The 1944 Act followed and responded to the evidence of government commissions, trade unions and teachers' organizations that existing arrangements were socially divisive and wasteful. The comprehensive reorganization can be seen as developing from a groundswell of popular opinion that the post-1944 system was not achieving the hopes of the majority of the British public for equality of educational opportunity (see Parkinson, 1970; Rubinstein and Simon, 1973).

The picture that emerges, then, from the social conscience theorists is quite clear. The development of state social welfare intervention is to be seen as resting on and stemming from the growth of social conscience among the population in general. This collective conscience promotes a rational and moral response from government and state in the enactment and implementation of social policies which are themselves cumulative, beneficent and irreversible. The social conscience thesis is founded on a belief in a powerful, well-informed and rational state, the existence of which precludes the idea of continuing serious injustice.

AIMS AND FUNCTIONS OF STATE WELFARE

Implicit in the above description of social policy development are the social conscience theorists' views about the aims and functions of state welfare provision. For them the aims and functions of service provision are as unproblematic as the development of state welfare.

For Slack, they appear to be threefold: the prevention of suffering, premature death, or social ill; the protection of the sick and vulnerable from dangers and pressures which they cannot withstand; and the promotion of the good of the individual and society (Slack, 1966, p. 93). As we might expect, the social conscience approach – based on a consensus model of society rooted in a functionalist sociological orientation – brooks no conflict between the protection and prevention from ill of the individual, on the one hand, and the needs of society on the other. The assumption, implicit in this approach, is as follows. Society is characterized by a common core of values and a common set of goals; moreover, individuals and societal subsystems interrelate to achieve these functional prerequisites of society. The needs of individuals and society are, therefore, likely to be essentially similar.

However, even in a society which is essentially harmonious and just, problems such as poverty and disease occur. Many such problems are perceived of as having roots in temporary societal malfunctions, and the aims of state welfare are to rectify these diswelfares which exist in an otherwise fair society.

The Citizenship and Social Welfare Approach

Another reformist perspective on social welfare, rooted in reformist approaches to the state, is the citizenship and social welfare approach. Like the social conscience approach it sees state intervention in welfare as developing from a consensus on the need for such intervention. Unlike that approach, however, it sees that societal consensus as having been forged out of a process which included conflict. Like the previous approach it sees state social welfare as functioning to ameliorate diswelfares. But unlike that approach it sees the creation of an equality in social rights as legitimizing inequality in the wider society. The work of T. H. Marshall and C. A. R. Crosland will be considered here although a number of writers share all or part of the perspective (see, for example, Parker, 1975 for a thoroughgoing attempt to study social policy development from this perspective).

SOCIAL WELFARE DEVELOPMENT

In a seminal article entitled *Citizenship and Social Class* (Marshall, 1963), the late T. H. Marshall outlines an explanatory model of the development of state welfare which has had considerable influence in the area of social policy studies. His model owes much to the hypothesis, promoted by the nineteenth-century economist Alfred Marshall, that there is a kind of human equality associated with the concept of full membership of a community. Full membership of a community, or society, is – according to T. H. Marshall – contingent on the individual's possession of three sets of citizen rights: civil rights, political rights and social rights. In contemporary society such rights may be defined in the following way:

civil rights   are those rights concerned with individual liberty and include freedom of speech and thought, the right to own private property and the right to justice;

political rights are primarily those rights of participation in the political process of government, either as an elector or as an elected member of an assembly;

social rights   cover a whole range of rights from the right to a modicum of economic security through to the right to share in the heritage and living standards of a civilized society. (Marshall, 1963, p. 74)

State provided social welfare is seen by Marshall as part of the package of social rights which are one element of the rights of citizenship. In feudal Britain, land owners may have possessed all three elements of citizenship rights. In the medieval towns all three sets of rights may have permeated down through the social class structure. The development of a complete package of rights on a national scale embracing all classes is, however, a relatively recent development. In approximate terms, the formative period for the development of each set of rights can be set in one of the three last centuries. In the eighteenth century civil rights, especially those of equality before the law, were extended to wider sections of the population than had hitherto been the case. In the nineteenth century and early twentieth century political rights, previously limited to the aristocracy were extended first to the middle classes, then to working class men and finally to women. In the twentieth century social rights, previously available only to the destitute (and then on unfavourable conditions through the operation of the Poor Law), were extended to working people – in the form of selective social welfare provisions – and then, through the creation of a universalist welfare state, to the whole population (Marshall, 1963, pp. 77–82).

Thus, this approach might have been seen as presenting a unilinear and inevitable development of state social welfare. Such an interpretation, however, does the citizenship and social welfare approach less than justice. The roots of citizenship rights are traced back through history and the extension of these rights seen as extensions in the British democratic tradition. However, social rights – including state welfare provision – are seen as having emerged out of a democratic process, ultimately leading to consensus over social and political affairs but which has included conflict between classes and genders.

Marshall argues that the movement for equality of political rights, including Chartism in the nineteenth century and suffragism in the early twentieth century, developed from a determination to extend the rights of all citizens beyond equality of civil rights. Similarly, the establishment of universal political rights and enfranchisement, contributing, for example, to the election of working people's representatives to Parliament, aided the struggle for equality of social rights. These social rights, enshrined in welfare state policies, included the right to a modicum of economic security (through the income maintenance system), the right to share in the living standards of a civilized society (through policies of full employment and the health system) and the right to share a common cultural heritage (through the education system) (Marshall, 1963, pp. 84–6).

Although the extension of rights at each stage has been accompanied by political struggle to achieve those rights, the effect has been, at every stage, to mould a new consensus on rights reaching its climax in the extension of social rights. This pinnacle having been achieved, social rights (education, health and income maintenance rights, for example) facilitate the individual's ability to utilize fully his or her civil and political rights.

This citizenship–democracy model is given substance by Crosland. In a speech reproduced in his collection of essays, *Socialism Now* (Crosland, 1974), he locates the movement for comprehensive secondary education within Marshall's citizenship model.

> I believe . . . this represents a strong and irresistible pressure on British society to extend the rights of citizenship. Over the past three hundred years these rights have been extended first to personal liberty then to political democracy and later to social welfare. Now they must be further extended to educational equality. (Crosland, 1974, p. 194)

Implicit in this explanation of the development of state welfare intervention are reformist views of the state and government. The consensus on rights has roots in a democratic tradition. It may, at times, have been forged out of struggle and conflict but once that consensus, however created, has emerged governments must inevitably respond to an irresistible groundswell of opinion and the state machinery must aid the implementation of social rights.

AIMS AND FUNCTIONS OF SOCIAL WELFARE

The emphasis of the citizenship approach on the creation of equality of rights may lead the reader to speculate that this approach presents the aims of state social welfare as including the achievement of material equality through redistribution. On the contrary, Marshall's analysis sees the equality of social status accorded to all by the rights of citizenship as legitimizing economic inequalities inherent in British capitalist society. It is no accident that the growth of citizen rights coincided with the growth of capitalism as an economic and social system. The economic rights which form part of a citizen's civil rights are seen as indispensable in a market economy, for they permit the individual to engage, through the right to buy, own and sell, in economic struggle for the maximization of profit. Political rights may have redressed some of the power imbalance between the social classes of capitalist society but social rights in peripherally modifying the pattern of social inequality have had the paradoxical, but functional, effect of making the social class system less vulnerable to change (Marshall, 1963). They have had such an effect because they have accorded community membership to all – and thus have given all a stake in capitalist society – without effecting any fundamental redistribution in income or wealth. Social welfare has raised the level of the lowest (through income maintenance schemes, education, health care systems and the like), but redistribution of resources has been horizontal rather than vertical (that is, within social classes rather than between them). In the British welfare state, inequality persists but the possession by all citizens of a package of social rights has created a society in which no *a priori* valuations are made on the basis of social class or social status. For Marshall, then, the aims and functions of state welfare policies and service provision include: the incorporation of all as members of the societal community; the modification of the most excessive and debilitating inequalities of British society; but the legitimization of wider and more fundamental inequalities through this process of incorporation.

For Crosland, also, the aims and functions of welfare state policy are not primarily those of equality through redistribution. For him, social equality cannot be held to be the ultimate purpose of the social services (Crosland, 1956, p. 148). Rather, the aims are to provide relief of social distress and the correction of social needs. Inequalities will be lessened as a result, but the creation of equality is, at most, a subsidiary objective (Crosland, 1956). Indeed, in an earlier contribution to the debate on welfare, Crosland makes his views on welfare state aims even more explicit:

> The object of social services is to provide a cushion of security . . . Once that security has been provided further advances in the national income should normally go to citizens in the form of free income to be spent as they wish and not to be taxed away and then returned in the form of some free service determined by the fiat of the state. (Crosland, 1952, p. 63)

The state, in creating a welfare state in the 1940s had, in Crosland's view, substantially, if not completely, satisfied the need and demand for universal and full membership of the societal community. The objects of state welfare provision are to cushion insecurity and to ameliorate excessive inequality rather than to promote equality. The idea of state welfare as the cushion or shock absorber of the inequalities of capitalist society is one which will also be found in some of the Marxist views on welfare. The difference is that – while Marshall, Crosland and others see this function as an appropriate one – for the Marxist writers it forms part of their critique of state welfare.

Feminism, Reformism and Welfare

A number of twentieth-century feminist thinkers, writers and activists have developed views on welfare which appear to have their roots in both feminism and reformism. Their views on welfare are feminist inasmuch as they are concerned with the improvement of the position of women in society. They are reformist inasmuch as they appear to have deep roots in a social democratic view of state, government and society.

SOCIAL WELFARE DEVELOPMENT

All strands of contemporary feminist writing on welfare underline the fact that dominant understandings of welfare development understate, if they state at all, the influence of women on the development of state welfare (Dale and Foster, 1986). Women as individuals, or indeed as organized groups, appear to have been substantially hidden from the history of welfare by most of the social welfare literature. During the last decade feminist writers have disinterred the contribution of women to welfare development from the graves of history to which it had been consigned (Wilson, 1977; 1981; Banks, 1981; Dale and Foster, 1986).

Interestingly, that process of excavation has unearthed a number of quite distinct strands of analysis of welfare development and function. One of those strands, perhaps best represented in the contemporary literature by Banks (1981), elucidates the links between one tendency in feminist thought and reformist ideas of state and government.

Commenting on the success of early-twentieth-century feminist campaigns on suffrage, pay, and welfare, Banks relies on an understanding of the state deeply rooted in social democratic theory. These early-century campaigns were substantially successful, she argues, because of an alliance between feminism and the newly formed Labour Party (1981, p. 164). That alliance was created as a result of pressure on the Labour Party to forge a new consensus on the role and status of women in society which was cemented by the implementation of legislation to improve women's position in 1920s Britain. Informed argument, then, initiated by 'an articulate and socially well connected group of women' (Lewis, 1973) and supported by other forms of persuasion, 'was to make the Labour Party receptive to many policies that were also of importance to the feminists' (Banks, 1981). The implementation of those policies should therefore be seen, from this perspective, as illustrating a relationship between civil society, state and government based on the subordination of government to civil society and the subordination of the state to government.

Dale and Foster (1986) remind us that such a reformist strategy was at the heart of the campaigns of most early-century feminist campaigns for welfare.

Their activities might include demonstrations, but they

concentrated on peaceful persuasion, building alliances with (male) MPs, other organisations and lobbying patiently behind the scenes. (1986, p. 5)

One tendency within feminist thought and action on welfare, then, may be comfortably accommodated within a reformist approach to welfare development. Most early-century activists and some contemporary writers see progress in welfare, and elsewhere, as stemming from the building of a new consensus on the position of women in society. That consensus building presumed a process including the promotion of informed arguments, lobbying and alliance building leading to the response of government and state through legislation. Such a tradition reached its zenith in the implementation of sex discrimination legislation (Equal Pay Act, 1970; Sex Discrimination Act, 1975), the establishment of an Equal Opportunities Commission and the burgeoning of a reformist feminist literature (e.g. Novarra, 1980; most EOC publications).

AIMS AND FUNCTIONS OF WELFARE

Unlike their Marxist or socialist feminist counterparts (see pp. 91–2), feminists in this tradition conceive the aims and functions of welfare as aiding the aims of feminism. For the early feminists, such as those in the Women's Co-operative Guild, state intervention to provide family allowances, or maternity and welfare services, represented a positive if not total contribution to the achievement of welfare and equality of status. They did so, in part, because they would liberate working class women particularly from the financial necessity of paid (often underpaid) work and thus allow them to devote themselves more fully to their primary task of child and family care. Though this may be anathema to many contemporary feminists it was regarded by many as releasing working women from one part of the dual burden of paid work and home work. State welfare, then, for early reformist feminists would function to ameliorate the negative features of working class women's 'enforced' participation in the workforce.

State welfare would also function, as the movement for endowment of motherhood identified, to create improved conditions in which women might carry out their role as mothers and child-carers. It would function to

> lighten the burden of those who have families to support, or to create the conditions in which mothers can give the best service they are capable of to work which is truly of national importance. (Royden, 1918, quoted in Loney, Boswell and Clarke, 1984)

The aims of state welfare for these feminists, then were coterminous with the aims of a feminism which did not seek to question the traditional wisdom that women's appropriate role was that of mother and houseworker rather than that of paid worker. The dawning of the welfare state may be regarded from this perspective as representing the pinnacle of feminist achievement:

> in it women have become ends in themselves and not merely means to the ends of men. The welfare state has been both cause and consequence of the second great change by which women have moved . . . from rivalry with men to a new recognition of their unique value as women. (Brittain, 1953, p. 224)

Later welfare policies concerned with women are seen, in this perspective, as promoting similar aims and goals and are recognized as having achieved these by means similar to the earlier ones.

The Industrial State and Welfare Approach

The citizenship approach, as we have seen, permits in a somewhat limited way for a dialectical relationship between consensus and conflict in the development of state welfare. The industrial state and welfare approach proposes a deterministic functionalist explanation of that process. The development of industrial societies inevitably leads to the development of welfare states and those welfare states function, and are intended to function, to service the industrial states which gave them birth. This approach draws on the work of Kerr (Kerr *et al.*, 1962), the convergence theorists Dunning and Hopper

(Dunning and Hopper, 1966), the American economist John Kenneth Galbraith (Galbraith, 1972) and others. It finds its clearest expression, in its application to social welfare, in the work of Willensky and Lebaux (Willensky and Lebaux, 1965).

This view of welfare is set within a wider model of society and state which seeks to explain the formation of social structures in all societies and is often referred to as convergence theory. As we have seen in Chapter 2, it is a functionalist approach which proposes that the most important factor influencing the development of social structures and social institutions is neither political consensus nor political conflict. Rather, it is the development of industrial technology which influences societies' institutional patterns. In a nutshell, 'given the decision to have modern industry, much of what happens is inevitable and the same' (Galbraith, 1972, p. 396). Although there exists a societal interplay between the forces of uniformity (industrial development) and the forces of diversity (including ideology), it is the logic of industrialism which is the stronger. Consequently all industrialized societies are likely to develop, at similar points in their industrial development, similar support and maintenance systems. All industrial societies, for example, are likely to develop well-organized education systems in order to create an appropriately trained workforce, and so on.

If industrial development is the core prerequisite of societies, how then does welfare develop and what functions does it perform in service of this prime functional requirement?

SOCIAL WELFARE DEVELOPMENT

We can describe the relationship between industrial society and the development of state welfare in the following way:

(1) As societies developed an industrial base, so the relatively simple exchange relationships of agrarian social formations were replaced by more complex industrial economies. The industrial state became a key regulator of economic relationships in a way that had hitherto not been the case (Kerr *et al.*, 1962). As the self-employed farmers, craftsmen and the like were replaced by industrial workers so employment for a wage

became the dominant form of economic exchange between workers and employers. This transformation of the labour force into industrial wage labourers also imposed a clear distinction between those at work and those not at work. Problems of earnings interruption, whether caused by sickness or unemployment, became acute and precipitated state provision of income maintenance schemes.

Such schemes as those introduced in Britain by Liberal governments at the start of this century had the effect of maintaining workers at least at a subsistence level until they were reintroduced into the workforce. Income maintenance legislation of the 1940s can be seen from this perspective as a reaction to changed employment patterns and industrial processes resulting from wartime devastation. Similarly, the earnings related unemployment benefit introduced in 1966 might be seen as a development occasioned by Britain's rapid technological development and automation which generated the unemployment of those with defunct skills and the redeployment of those same people, at some future time, in new jobs demanding new skills.

(2) Industrial society also requires increased levels of formal education. Education policies can, as a result, be seen as acting as the handmaidens of industrialism. Early industrial processes demanded a basic grounding in the skills of numeracy and literacy. Mass elementary education, introduced as a result of the 1902 Education Act, therefore became an imperative. As industrial technology developed so did policies on education. The 1944 Education Act created a secondary education system intended to train the personnel of a developing industrial society: the industrializing elites (in the grammar schools); the technical workers (in the technical schools); and the industrial proletariat (in the modern schools). Comprehensive reorganization might be seen as a policy innovation, by the state, to educate an appropriate and flexible workforce for a Britain in the throes of a technological revolution.

(3) Industrial societies also tend to create high levels of social disorganization and social dislocation. Such disorganization and dislocation was evident in the initial stage of industrialization and at later points of development. The erstwhile agrarian

workers' relocation in the industrial towns of the Industrial
Revolution separated them from the traditional informal
networks of support provided by family, kin, the church, etc.
Out-migration of workers from depressed industrial areas, at
various points of this century, and their relocation in the newer
factory towns are said to have had a similar effect.

   In such a complex society, personal social service agencies
were developed – initially benevolent societies with welfare
agencies and latterly state organized social service agencies – to
replace the informal networks which had been lost (see Mishra,
1981, for a rehearsal of these arguments). Willensky and
Lebaux clearly adopt this perspective on social welfare
development in North America. They trace the impact of
industrialization on American society. Early industrialization is
argued to have effected changes in the family, with the
experience of social dislocation leading to, for example:
abandonment of the aged, plus a greater incidence of marriage
breakdown; changes in systems of economic support; and
changes in educational demands, all of which precipitated the
development of welfare systems to solve such problems. Later,
industrialization led to demands for more educational and
industrial specialization and to higher levels of social and
geographical mobility. These problems, too, are said to have
prompted the development of statutory welfare services
(Willensky and Lebaux, 1965, chs 3 and 4).

   The development of state welfare is, then, in this approach
seen as a functional accompaniment to industrial development.
Once industrial states exist, the creation of welfare states within
them is almost inevitable. Government and state simply
respond to the logic of industrialization. State welfare develops
as industrial technology proceeds.

AIMS AND FUNCTIONS OF SOCIAL WELFARE

The industrial state and welfare approach is based on essentially
functionalist premisses. As such it sees the state provision of
welfare as contributing to the functional requirements of
society. Welfare is seen as facilitating the social cohesion of
society and as especially useful for industrial societies at times

of rapid economic or industrial change. Specifically, welfare provision forms part of the industrial state's intention to achieve system integration and social integration and has the effect of doing just that.

For instance, social welfare may be argued to contribute to system integration by working to integrate a number of temporarily mal-integrating subsystems at points of accelerated societal change. At the earliest point of industrialization, in Britain in the 1940s, and in the mid 1960s the education subsystem might be regarded as having been out of harmony with the economy. A certain kind of labour force was necessary for these particular phases in the development of industrial Britain and the existing education systems were unable to provide a force with appropriate skills. In consequence, according to this approach, policies of intervention were developed to integrate social subsystems around a core requirement. Similarly, in instances of dysfunction between a particular phase of industrial development – say automation – on the one hand and labour force skills or numbers, on the other, income maintenance policies ease the process of harmonizing the apparently contradictory requirements of the industrial macro-system and the employment subsystem.

State social welfare also contributes, we are told, to a process of social integration. Developments in industrial technology lead to the sorts of social dislocation we have described earlier. Social welfare provision, especially in the area of personal social services, can be seen as aiding social cohesion and preventing social fractures within a society which, at particular points of its development, risks disintegration and fracture.

The Capitalist State and Welfare

Marxist approaches to welfare are explicitly linked to Marxist views about the state in capitalist countries. However, as we have seen in Chapter 2, Marxist views of the state differ in essential respects. As we shall now see, Marxist approaches to the development and to the aims and functions of state welfare exhibit similar differences of emphasis.

SOCIAL WELFARE DEVELOPMENT

There is no better place to start a discussion on the development of state welfare than with the views of Marx himself. Marx's contribution to the literature on state welfare development takes, of course, the form of prediction rather than description as state intervention in this field was largely absent during the nineteenth century. For Marx, the development of total welfare which provided for the needs of people was impossible under capitalism. However, Marx's argument, in some of his writings (see Marx, 1967, vol. 1, for example), that partial welfare which provided for the satisfaction of some of the needs of people (and working class people in particular) was possible points up an ambiguity or duality in Marx's thought. In other words, Marx saw that piecemeal social reforms might meet some human needs while, at the same time, his overall system determinism led him to question the extent of change possible.

The example most referred to in this respect is Marx's analysis of early welfare development in the form of the Factory Acts (1833–67) (see Mishra, 1975, for a detailed discussion of Marx's views in this respect and Marx, 1967, for the original argument). Marx was in no doubt that the Factory Acts constituted a serious modification of the capitalist economic and social system: the regulation of working hours posed a restriction to the employer's ability to exploit the worker. This development is seen by him as resulting from the class struggle between the working class and the ruling class, 'the outcome of a protracted civil war, more or less veiled' (Marx, 1967, vol. 1, p. 307). Additionally, a third grouping was involved. The landed aristocracy, perceiving a conflict of interests between themselves and the industrial bourgeoisie, became instrumental allies of the working class and paradoxically a significant part of the movement to enact reform measures.

What emerges, then, is an analysis which suggests that the capitalist state intervenes to develop welfare initiatives and therefore acts against the interests of industrial capitalism if working class pressure is significant enough and threatening enough and/or if there are divisions of interest in the capitalist class. Here we have, then, an analysis which exposes the duality in Marx's views of the capitalist state referred to in an earlier chapter (pp. 45–56). Although the dominant understanding of the state, in Marx's writing, is that it is simply an instrument of the dominant class (see Marx and Engels, 1967), there is also a strand of thought which suggests that the state is, or might be, relatively autonomous from the class structure. What then of later Marxist approaches? Mandel's approach (Mandel, 1968) is almost pure system determinism. It presents us with a very simple picture: developments in state welfare should be seen as reflecting changes in the nature of capitalism. In the early stages of industrial capitalism state welfare was largely absent but, where it did exist, arose from a need to bolster an economy based on entrepreneurial capitalism. Sanitation and housing policies were developed to ensure the existence of a healthy working population housed in the proximity of industrial work places. Very little more state intervention was necessary, certainly not in the economy, as entrepreneurial capitalism would respond, almost instinctively, to market forces.

However, as the entrepreneurial capitalism of the nineteenth century developed into the corporate capitalism of the twentieth century the state was, perforce, drawn into social and economic intervention to aid the profitability of capitalism in its new form. The capital intensive operations of large corporations require a stability of consumption of their products: corporate capitalism responds rather more slowly to the forces of the market. To ensure stability of consumption the state intervenes and provides systems of social insurance, social security and unemployment benefit. The worker whose earnings have been interrupted can, therefore, continue to consume.

Moreover, corporate capitalism's drive to increase productivity, consumption and therefore profit leads to the introduction of policies for mass health and educational services so that the productivity and productive life of the worker might be increased.

Baran and Sweezy (1968) construct a similarly deterministic

model. For them, one of the features of modern capitalism is that the productive potential of capitalism constantly outstrips demand for its products. What is needed, as a consequence, are policies which operate to stimulate demand and among these policies one might place state income maintenance policies.

State intervention in welfare, then, for Mandel and for Baran and Sweezy arises from the requirements of capitalism. It marks neither the end of capitalism (Powell, 1969) nor its transformation (Crosland, 1952). Rather it strengthens the power and wealth of the powerful and wealthy and marks but a new phase in capitalist development.

Saville's understanding of the development of welfare does, on the other hand, allow for a range of other significant formative influences as well as economic ones. He sees state welfare policies as having developed, in part at least, as a consequence of working class agitation for better standards of health, education, housing and economic security (Saville, 1957). However, he argues that, while working class struggle might be the engine of welfare development, those welfare provisions which emerge represent no more than the concessions which the capitalist class is prepared to make through its instrument, the state. Furthermore, the state permits only those concessions which are acceptable to the owners of capital and which contribute to economic efficiency and social stability.

Thus education and health policies might be seen to contribute to the creation of a workforce made more productive because of its possession of intellectual skills and good health. Education and personal social service policies might be argued to contribute to social stability by establishing social institutions which socialize working people into the values and norms of capitalist society.

The American writer O'Connor (1973) similarly views the state as the instrument of the capitalist class and state welfare as a development emerging from militant working class struggle. Notwithstanding this view of welfare development, O'Connor argues that the concessions won as a result of class struggle amount merely to the development of social policies which protect the interests of the owners of capital. State social welfare is precipitated by the agitation and struggle of the poor and working class but the policy forms which emerge illustrate the predisposition of the state to act as a handmaiden to a ruling class or elite. As a consequence of this analysis, the American war on poverty of the 1960s is seen as having been precipitated by the spread of civil rights and welfare rights militancy of the period. However, the policy innovations developed were of a type which reinforced the values of a capitalist society, dependent for its continuation on social and economic inequality (O'Connor, 1973, pp. 150–75). The capitalist state, in its activities in welfare, as elsewhere, acts as the 'class conscious directorate' of the ruling class.

More recently, however, some Marxist writers have reacted against the bias towards system determinism in earlier Marxist approaches to welfare. The development of state welfare and its aims and functions are contextualized within an analysis of society and state which emphasizes the contradictions inherent in capitalist society and the possibility of some degree of state autonomy from the capitalist class.

Among the more significant contributions to this strand of Marxist thinking about welfare is the work of Gough (1975; 1979) and Ginsburg (1979). In modern capitalist society, state welfare interventions are seen as having emerged out of quite different formative processes. The state is seen as exhibiting, at different times, different degrees of relative autonomy from a capitalist class.

Gough, for example, argues that some major welfare interventions by the state have been made as a result of ruling class self-interest. However, at other times, the threat or actuality of popular discontent and mass struggle have forced the state to act in the interests of a wider constituency than the ruling class. At yet other times a congruence of interest between the two major social classes has occurred and specific welfare interventions have emerged out of this convergence of interests. The development of mass education by capitalist societies is seen as resulting from capitalism's need for an educated workforce: state provision of education can, therefore, be seen as illustrating the state's handmaiden role to capitalism at a particular historical point and in particular circumstances.

The presence of popular discontent and the threat of mass struggle can be seen as precipitating such reforms as the 1911 Unemployment Insurance Act, and such state action can be viewed as demonstrating the state's capability of acting in the interests of sections of the population other than the ruling class. Health, education and income maintenance policies – developed during and since the 1940s – can often be regarded as stemming from a congruence of interest between capital and labour: capital requiring a healthy, educated and physically efficient workforce and labour demanding access to a civilized quality and standard of life (Gough, 1975, pp. 72–6; 1979, pp. 64–74).

Similarly, Ginsburg appears to suggest that the welfare state emerges as an uneasy resolution of the usually contradictory forces of capital and labour.

> the welfare state is not . . . an untrammelled achievement of the working class in struggle . . . nor is it viewed as an institution shaped largely by the demands and requirements of the capitalist economy. The welfare state has been formed around the contradictions and conflicts of capital develop- ment. (Ginsburg, 1979, p. 2)

Social security policies, for instance, can therefore be regarded as having developed to aid the reproduction of a surplus labour force but also, if secondarily, to mitigate poverty. State social policy develops out of contradictions, and the state, in welfare, acts in a way relatively, if not totally, autonomous of the interests of the ruling class.

A somewhat different argument is constructed by Offe who sees state welfare developing, in some part at least, because of the heterogeneous nature of ruling classes. He sees the state as sandwiched between two inherently antagonistic influences (capital and labour). Because the state generates large amounts of income from private capital, and because senior state personnel have similar social provenance to the owners of capital, the state is predisposed to protect the interests of the capitalist class. Much social welfare intervention (including health, education and income maintenance) should be seen as having developed because the state has acted to promote those interests. However, according to Offe, the state operates in a tension between the power of capital and the power of labour and, when it has been confronted on welfare (as on other issues) by mass political action (or the threat of such action), it has and does display a degree of relative autonomy from the capitalist class. Policies which emerge at such times are likely to emerge because of – rather than despite – working class action, are likely to be more concerned with the interests of the whole population than policies developed in other circumstances, and are most likely to have emerged during periods of Labour government (Offe, 1982).

Marxist writers differ, then, in the emphasis they place on the needs and interests of capital, on the one hand, and the activity of the working class on the other, in the process of welfare development. They differ, also, in their assessment of the extent to which the capitalist state might be seen as autonomous of ruling class interests. There is a consequent difference in emphasis in these writers' views about the aims and functions of state welfare. All are agreed that state welfare functions to reproduce the social and economic relations of capitalist society. There is, however, significant disagreement about the extent to which welfare policies might also paradoxically function to provide some degree of welfare for their recipients. It is to a presentation of these different accounts that we now turn.

AIMS AND FUNCTIONS OF STATE WELFARE

Welfare as the handmaiden of capitalism   For a number of authors, the aims and functions of welfare are conceptually unproblematic. If state welfare developed out of corporate capitalism's need to provide stability of consumption and increased productivity and profit then welfare aims and functions are obvious and clear. For Mandel, as for Baran and Sweezy, the system that created welfare also determines its functions. Twentieth-century corporate capitalism is argued to require stability of demand for its products and, once demand has been stabilized, increased productivity of those products. Welfare meets these twin demands by providing a modicum of

economic security so that, even in unemployment, people can
continue to consume, and also by developing policies in
education and health which contribute to increased productivity
and to an increase in the productive life of workers. Welfare for
these writers, therefore, performs a servicing function for the
capitalist economy.

Saville and O'Connor develop and broaden this analysis.
Saville, notwithstanding claims that working class struggle has
played some part in welfare development, sees capitalism as
having two main preoccupations. These preoccupations with
economic efficiency and social stability are catered for by
welfare which acts as a 'shock absorber' for capitalist society.
Like Mandel and Baran and Sweezy, Saville sees state policies
in the areas of education, health and income maintenance
contributing to economic efficiency and stability. Unlike them
he also perceives of capitalism's need for social stability and
legitimacy. Consequently welfare, by providing a measure of
economic security, education, health care and the like,
contributes especially in times of unrest, or potential unrest, to
system integration. It does so, incorporating a potentially
radical and rebellious working class into capitalist society, by
providing, albeit reluctantly, an extension of social rights. The
possession of these social rights erodes working class radicalism,
evokes social obligations to maintain society relatively unchanged, and effects the social stability and legitimacy required
for the perpetuation of capitalism. (Saville, 1957, p. 11)

O'Connor also attributes twin and sometimes contradictory
aims to capitalism. For him, they are accumulation and
legitimization. Welfare is seen as functioning to achieve both of
these aims. State welfare policies are seen primarily as
legitimizing mechanisms: the state involves itself in expenditure
on projects and services which are required to maintain social
harmony. Social work, community work and the like are
provided by the state to promote conformity and value
congruence in a society characterized by value conflicts and
potential class warfare. Anti-poverty programmes, such as the
American 'War on Poverty', were introduced as palliatives at a
time of militant unrest about the plight of the urban poor. The
programmes themselves, however, implicitly saw the problems

of poverty as caused by the fecklessness and deficient moral values of the poor. O'Connor therefore sees such programmes as functioning to legitimize the structural inequality of capitalist society by attempting to change the values of the poor.

State welfare, though primarily contributing to a process of legitimization, may also, according to O'Connor, contribute to the process of capital accumulation. Obvious examples here are education and income maintenance policies (O'Connor, 1973, pp. 169–75).

State welfare intervention is, for the writers mentioned above, intended to serve as a handmaiden to capitalist society. It functions to service the economic needs or the social needs of capitalism, or both. The state in providing welfare services and developing welfare policies exhibits relatively little, if any, autonomy from the ruling class or elite whose interests state social welfare serves.

The contradictory nature of welfare and relative autonomy The system determinism of Mandel, Baran and Sweezy, Saville and O'Connor is somewhat modified in the writings of Gough, Ginsburg and Leonard. For these writers the development of state welfare is rooted in contradiction and manifests some degree of relative autonomy, however small, for the state. Similarly, the aims and functions of welfare are also contradictory. The prime function of state welfare is, it is argued, undoubtedly to service and reproduce capitalist economic relations and capitalist values: '[the social security system] is concerned with reproducing a reserve army of labour, the patriarchal family and the disciplining of the labour force' (Ginsburg, 1979, p. 2).

However, welfare does function – albeit secondarily – to provide a modicum of security or the 'partial welfare' to which Marx referred. So that while public housing policy is 'directed towards regulating the consumption of a vital commodity for the reproduction of the labour force' it is, albeit secondarily and contingently, 'an attempt to provide secure and adequate accommodation for the working class' (Ginsburg, 1979, p. 2).

Gough argues that state welfare policies have the paradoxical functions of being both control and containment of the

working class and also providing the satisfaction of some of the
needs of that class (Gough, 1979, p. 66).

What Leonard (Bean and MacPherson, 1983) describes is a
'dialectic of welfare' – its ability to service capitalism and
provide some measure of welfare to its recipients at one and the
same time – is at the core of these writers' work. For them, the
exact form which welfare takes and the balance of interests
served by welfare is dependent, in large part, on the balance of
class forces at the time of welfare development. Welfare
policies may function in more or less progressive ways
dependent on the relative strength and stability of capital, on
the one hand, and labour on the other. The state's relative
autonomy from a capitalist class is more pronounced at times
when that class, or fractions of it, are most vulnerable. Policies
developed by the state at such times, like the early social
insurance provisions, function more obviously to provide at
least partial welfare than do policies developed when capital is
more stable. The functions of welfare are always significantly
constrained and directed by the relationship of the state to the
owners of capital. However, the conflict between the interests
of capital and the interests of labour are reflected in the
contradictory aims and functions of social policy.

Significant differences of emphasis exist, then, in Marxist
writing on welfare. Specifically:

(1) welfare development is seen either as a result of political
struggle between social classes (real or threatened) or as
stemming from the needs of capitalist society:

(2) the state is conceptualized either as merely the 'class
conscious directorate' of the ruling class, or, in other Marxist
writings, as relatively autonomous from that class, though
significantly constrained by its relationship to that class to act
in its interests;

(3) the aims and functions of welfare are consequently seen
as either to service capitalism and ensure system integration and
social integration, or, on the other hand, to include sometimes
contradictory goals.

Feminism, Marxism and Welfare

Over the last decade or so there has been the growth of a perspective on welfare which applies and supplements Marxist understandings of the state and welfare to a consideration of the impact of the welfare state on women. Like other feminist perspectives it reintroduces women on to the stage of welfare development and reminds us of the role played by feminists and other women in the development of informal and formal welfare systems. Its particular and unique contribution, however, lies in how it theorizes the aims and functions of state welfare.

AIMS AND FUNCTIONS OF STATE WELFARE

For feminists attempting to marry the understandings of feminism and Marxism, a particularly difficult marriage according to one writer (Hartman, 1981), state welfare functions to further entrench women's inferior position in a society characterized by gender as well as class inequalities (Wilson, 1977; 1980).

From this perspective, the capitalist state acts to define femininity and appropriate roles for women in a particular way. State definitions of the role and attributes of women presume that women will normally be members of families in which they are dependent, as wives or daughters, on men (Ginsburg, 1979). It is necessary or functional that this should be so in order that women may be socialized into their conventional primary task as adults, that of reproducing – biologically and socially – the workforce (Wilson, 1977, p. 8).

The welfare state in general, and specific social policies, are seen as key instruments in maintaining and reproducing women's position in a capitalist society (Wilson, 1977; Ginsburg, 1979). Income maintenance policies reinforce the idea and the actuality of women's dependence on men and on their role as home workers (see Ginsburg, 1979). Education socializes women into their future roles as wives and mothers (see Wilson, 1977; Deem, 1978; 1980; Delamont, 1980). Social work polices families in order to ensure that appropriate socialization functions are carried out (Handler, 1973; Wilson, 1977; Donzelot, 1980).

The welfare state, according to Wilson, is 'no less than the state organisation of domestic life' (1977, p. 9). It is a set of policies and institutions which helps maintain women in their role as reproducers of the workforce, dependent on men. It elevates their role as home workers and denigrates their contribution as paid workers. It functions ideologically to support and reinforce the conventional nuclear family in capitalist society. It provides legitimacy for the exploitation and oppression of women within families.

The aims and functions of welfare are, thus, seen as deeply inimical to the aims and functions of a feminism which seeks to liberate women from the fetters of a material reality and an ideology based on gender inequality, exploitation and oppression.

Radical Right Views of Welfare

The views of the radical right on welfare, associated with promotion of a market economy, have enjoyed considerable exposure in the last five years or so. The election, in 1979, of a government apparently committed to the dismantling of state welfare had contributed to a crisis of legitimacy for state provided welfare. Like some of the Marxists, the theorists of the radical right – among them Hayek, Friedman, Peacock and Powell – have constructed a powerful critique of welfare. This critique, however, is accompanied by clearly presented prescriptions for state involvement in welfare. It is intended, therefore, to review how this approach explains the development of welfare, what it sees as the functions of state welfare, and what such an analysis implies for state involvement in welfare.

The Development of State Welfare

Writers of the 'radical right' see the development of state welfare as an unfortunate occurrence. For them, almost all state intervention in social and economic affairs is to be regretted. Following Hayek (Hayek, 1949; 1980), the prophets of the new right see the natural state of man as one in which he is free from regulation by the state (Hayek, 1980) and free to express his natural individualism (Hayek, 1949). Such freedom from state regulation and individualism presumes the existence of a measure of inequality in society but, for these writers, freedom and substantive equality stand in direct contradiction to each other and equality must be sacrificed in the service of freedom (see George and Wilding, 1985, pp. 21–41, and Mishra, 1984, pp. 26–64).

If state intervention in general is regarded as interfering with the natural order, how do these writers explain its development? For Boyson the development of state welfare is to be understood by recourse to a sort of great man theory of history. The welfare state was created by well-intentioned, compassionate men (Boyson, 1971). Or, to put it another way, 'The welfare state has been fraudulently created by well meaning but misguided reformers capitalising on the aspirations of an unthinking public' (George and Wilding, 1985, pp. 36–42).

In essence, most writers who adopt this approach either follow Dicey (Dicey, 1962, p. 259) in arguing that state welfare developed as a result of the susceptibility of public opinion to the collectivist ideology of proponents of welfare, or argue that the collectivist ideas, which justify state regulation of social and economic relations through welfare, have their source in pressure groups or trade unions rather than in individuals. In any event, they concur with Hayek that this capturing of public opinion by collectivist ideals occurs because 'Though the characteristic methods of collective socialism have few defenders left in the West, its ultimate aims have lost little of their attraction' (Hayek, 1960, p. 256). Once public opinion has coalesced around the need for welfare the state, itself a creature of collectivists, acts to institutionalize state welfare in a systematic and ever larger network of welfare provision.

Aims and Functions of State Welfare

The aims and the functions of state welfare are seen, in this approach, as almost wholly detrimental to the development of a free society which protects freedom of choice and promotes innovation in industry, commerce and public life. Welfare functions to create a society in which individual responsibility for individual actions is denigrated. The effect of state welfare is social disruption, resource waste, economic inefficiency and the obliteration of individual freedom. State welfare is one, though not the only, step on the 'road to serfdom' (Hayek, 1944).

For Boyson, state welfare produces a 'broiler society' which saps the economic and spiritual incentive of people:

> A [welfare] state which does for its citizens what they can do for themselves is an evil state: and a state which removes all choice and responsibility from its people and makes them like broiler hens will create the irresponsible society. In such an irresponsible society no one cares, no one saves, no one bothers – why should they when the state spends all its energies taking money from the energetic, successful and thrifty to give to the idle, the failures and the feckless. (Boyson, 1971, p. 9)

State provision, in the areas of income maintenance, health, education, housing and the personal social services has the twin effects of removing freedom and thence responsibility, and of dampening down incentive.

The specific and detrimental functions of state welfare are, for the writers of the radical right, fourfold: state welfare provision promotes social grievances; it leads to wastage of resources; it causes economic inefficiency and it obliterates individual freedom.

Basically, the provision of welfare by the state promotes social disruption by translating needs into rights. The provision of universal services (health and education, for instance) takes no account of the extent of need for free services. Instead it provides blanket coverage for the minority of needy but also for the majority who could provide or finance services for themselves. Resources are therefore spread thinly and animosities are created between potential recipients of over-burdened state services (see Powell, 1972).

Free state services also lead to resource wastage. State social services, even if administered universally, have limited resources. However, at nil price demand is infinite. Provision of free state services therefore stimulates demand which cannot be met by insufficient resources. Service providers are unable to evaluate which demands are justifiable and which are not and the consequence is misallocation and waste of resources (Lejeune, 1970).

Resource waste is also engendered by consumer dissatisfaction with state services. Because services are administered centrally, consumers, it is argued, feel a sense of alienation from such externalized services. This alienation, however, is channelled into calls for inappropriate increase in resources. The state responds by providing more welfare to quieten 'a continual deafening chorus of complaint' (Powell, 1966, p. 20).

State social welfare also functions to promote inefficiency. Because central state services are, in effect, a government monopoly, sheltered from the price and profit mechanisms of the private market, there is a tendency towards profligate and unnecessary expenditure. Monopolistic social welfare also acts as a disincentive to innovation and experimentation which might lead to more efficient provision of social welfare (Hayek, 1973, vol.1, p. 14).

Equally importantly, state welfare provision acts to remove individual freedom and responsibility. The provision of state education, for instance, leads to the compulsion of parents to send their children to schools in particular areas and with uniform curricula. Parents are therefore denied the freedom to choose what sort of education provision might best meet their children's needs (see Friedman, 1962).

State welfare provision, then, represents backdoor state tyranny and socialism by stealth. It acts to interfere in and pervert the 'natural' workings of a market economy, to stimulate demands which it cannot meet and to strip the individual of freedom and responsibility. The result of such a trenchant analysis is, of course, a set of prescriptions for welfare which suggest a significant curtailment of state involvement in welfare and a reorientation of that involvement where it survives.

Prescriptions for Welfare

The ultimate aim for writers within this approach seems to be the dismantling of the welfare state. They look forward to a time when a market economy, generating economic growth and increased national wealth, will prevent extremes of inequality of wealth and income. In such a situation an efficient free enterprise system could dispense with state intervention; individuals and communities could and should provide and finance private welfare.

Even in our present state of development, the anti-collectivist writers argue for radical changes in state welfare provision. Specifically they argue for a reduction in the scope of the social services, a reduction in the level of financial state benefits (in part achieved by the present government), for local rather than central control of welfare and for substantial privatization of services. In short, they propose, in the words of George and Wilding, 'a residual, means tested, locally administered welfare state' (George and Wilding, 1985).

Presently, policies of subsidy and rent control in housing have a number of effects. These include housing shortage caused by reduction of price below that which current levels of supply and demand create (Lejeune, 1970, p. 32) and lack of individual freedom because rent control and housing subsidies make people subject to the decisions of others (Hayek, 1980, p. 344).

One solution provided by the anti-collectivists is the encouragement of home ownership which would reintroduce the ideal of individual freedom and re-establish the primacy of the market as a regulator of supply and demand (see Seldon, 1981, p. 71–86). Another, and complementary, solution is that housing subsidies, in whatever form, should be more rigorously means tested so that only the very worst off should benefit from state involvement in housing policy.

Similarly, health and education services, currently provided by the state, are ill conceived. Removal of price mechanisms leads to low quality service. The burden of taxation on the population, necessary to finance the services, acts as a general disincentive to work and innovation. The suppression of consumer choice in the services represents a denial of consumer freedom.

Proponents of anti-collectivist approaches therefore suggest the removal of state provided universal services in health and their replacement by compulsory insurance schemes (Harris, 1971, p. 76). In education, it is suggested that the state should provide financing for the service to ensure universal education coverage but should ensure freedom of consumer choice through a system of parental choice of schools (Boyson, 1971, p. 8).

The radical right then promote a view of welfare which dismisses the idea of a substantial role for government in the provision of welfare and which prescribes instead a minimalist and residual role.

Feminism, Neo-Liberalism and Welfare

Although substantially absent from contemporary feminist thought and writing on welfare, the early twentieth century saw the growth of a strand of feminism with links with liberal economic theory and philosophy. Although concerned with ending legal discrimination against women and promoting their rights to compete equally with men in the public world of work, it regarded state provision of welfare with great suspicion. For example, representatives of this strand of thinking opposed child allowances and free school meals on the grounds that families, and especially fathers, should bear the burden of their own responsibilities (Martin, 1913).

In its suspicion of state interventionism it reflected both *laissez-faire* economic principles and the moral principles of individual responsibility which formed one of the bases of ultra-right political thinking then as now.

The Welfare State in the 1980s

So far, this chapter has been devoted to describing different views of the development and functions of welfare particularly, though not exclusively, in the postwar period. As such it has concentrated on descriptions of how different approaches to welfare theorize the growth of welfare statism. Whether new conservative policies of the 1980s mark a radical break with an earlier consensus, or simply a restriction and reorientation of state involvement in welfare, there is a need to investigate how different approaches theorize the state of welfare in the 1980s.

As we have seen in Chapter 2 and in this chapter, reformist views of state and welfare regard decisions about state involvement in welfare (and indeed elsewhere in society) as dependent on a broad social consensus of values and ideas. Ideas are therefore seen as an important, perhaps the most important, force in moulding state policies. In Keynes's words, 'nothing is mightier than an idea whose time has come'. Implicit in this sort of analysis is the reformist explanation for the changes in scope and intent of welfare policies in the 1980s. If the state interventionism of previous decades was predicated on the strength of an informed social consensus of ideas, then may not the reduced or reoriented interventionism of the present decade be the result of a changed social consensus?

For the reformists, welfare is in crisis. That crisis is composed of cuts in welfare state services, and the perceived threat to their very existence is, as we have seen elsewhere, essentially reducible to the notion of 'a crisis of ideas'. New conservative ideas on state and welfare may have partly, or even largely, replaced earlier reformist ideas as the basis of societal consensus (see pp. 56–61). But, for the reformists, certain elements of the old consensus remain as an essential part of the consciousness of the British people. The present crisis, therefore, may be seen as a battle of ideas, a battle for the minds of the British people. For the reformists, the hope – indeed the intellectual conviction – is that reformist policies can be reinstituted on the political agenda if rational and convincing arguments are presented for them in the present battle of ideas (Kinnock, 1986).

Understanding the state of welfare is, as we have seen earlier in this text, not quite as simple for the industrial state and welfare theorists. If welfare interventions have necessarily been called forth at times of rapid technological change, in order to service the industrial system but also to maintain social cohesion at times of potential fracture, how should we understand the present reorientations and restrictions in welfare?

The inescapable conclusion from this perspective is that changes in the industrial process in Britain have been so momentous in the contemporary period that the present reorientation or restructuring of welfare is both a necessary and inevitable response to the industrial system. Growth in welfare may, understandably, have been a response to changes in the work process necessitating higher levels of education, health and mobility from the workforce. Welfare policies catering for economic needs of the frictionally unemployed can be seen as the inevitable concomitants of technological development which demanded a workforce with different skills. In a period when high levels of unemployment or underemployment appear to be the semi-permanent accompaniments of a struggling high technology industrial system, different inevitable responses are called forth by the industrial system. These contemporary responses to new circumstances arguably have no need to cater for the reproduction of a mass workforce and may, therefore, include cuts in services like education and health. Socialization functions, previously undertaken by welfare, can in this new situation arguably be more effectively administered by enhanced law enforcement. The logic of industrialism therefore still determines policy. That logic, however, has changed to take account of new circumstances.

Marxist writers quite clearly perceive there to be a crisis in welfare. The seeds of that crisis have been germinating for a number of years. We have seen that O'Connor (1973, pp. 7–12) argues that the capitalist state, through interventionist and other policies, must fulfil the twin functions of accumulation and legitimation. However, some Marxists have argued that, particularly during the 1970s, when Keynesian economic policies were no longer believed to be capable of generating economic growth, the problems of simultaneously fulfilling both functions became insuperable. In previous periods welfare functions may have legitimated the capitalist system of social organization and may indeed – in areas like education – have contributed to the accumulation process. Economic recession, however, has made the twin goals, which are always in tension, contradictory. In order to secure legitimation through extensive welfare services, levels of state expenditure have to be committed which threaten, in a slow growth economy, the process of capital accumulation, so that, according to O'Connor, state provision of welfare in the 1970s contributed to a fiscal crisis of the state, to a tendency for state expenditures to increase more rapidly than the means of financing them (O'Connor, 1973, p. 9).

The fiscal crisis of the 1970s has developed into a crisis of legitimacy (Habermas, 1976; Mishra, 1984) during the 1970s and 1980s as the rationale and existence of state welfare has been placed under close scrutiny by governments, radical right thinkers and the general population. The twin crises of finance and legitimacy have helped to create and reinforce a general, if not total, conviction that large scale state intervention in welfare is possible only in times of economic growth (fiscal crisis) and that, in any event, welfare functions to undermine economic health and moral strength (crisis of legitimacy).

Other Marxist contributions have, on the other hand, provided a less determinist view of the crisis in welfare (and the more general crisis surrounding state intervention). For them, although the state in its welfare functions may have – on the whole – represented the interests of capital because of 'the character of its leading personnel, the pressures exerted by an economically dominant class and . . . structural constraints' (Miliband, 1978, p. 74), this is less than the whole story.

This is so because the battle over state control is continuous 'since the battle is never finally won' (Miliband, 1969, p. 160). The battle over state intervention, indeed over the scope, nature and intent of welfare intervention, is an ideological battle. Control of the state, the scope of its interventionist activities, the ability of the state, through welfare and other areas, to represent the interests of wide sections of the population may depend significantly on the balance of social class forces at any one time. The state becomes an arena of social class struggle. State policies reflect that struggle. If contemporary state policies seem to be impregnated with the ideology of the radical right, then the right's control of the state needs to be 'understood in direct relation to alternative political formations attempting to occupy and control the same space' (Hall, 1979, p. 18).

The state, therefore, under its present management represents the interests of a dominant class (or class fraction) convinced of the need to restrict and reorientate welfare policies and provision. This may indeed constitute a crisis – even a crisis of legitimacy. However, there is no reason, in principle at least, why another social class should not displace the dominant class, if successful in ideological struggle, and control the state. Given such a possibility the crisis of welfare may be only temporary, at least in one respect. Presumably, from this perspective a progressive state would reprioritize state spending in order to provide more extensive welfare provision of a politically progressive nature.

As we might predict, the present state of welfare is regarded with some, if not complete, approval by the thinkers and writers of the radical right. For many (Hayek, 1944; 1980; Friedman, 1962; Powell, 1966; 1972; Boyson, 1971; Joseph and Sumption, 1979; etc.) it is a truism to argue that a welfare state is incapable of enhancing welfare. This individualist critique of welfare statism has been highlighted in this test (pp. 92–7) and elsewhere (Bosanquet, 1983; Seldon, 1981).

What is occurring in contemporary Britain, albeit too slowly for some, is the taming of the state, the reformulation of the notion of rights to mean individual family and community rights to provide individual, family and community welfare. Where that is not possible the formula permits the pump-priming of voluntary agencies in order to create a mixed economy of welfare. If this is a crisis it is to be welcomed by the radical right as it may presage the creation of a society in which the boundaries between state and civil society become fundamentally transformed.

Four very different approaches to welfare have been described in this chapter. Each of them draws, implicitly or explicitly, on particular models of state and society. Each of them also presents specific views of the state provision of social welfare. We proceed in the next chapter to a discussion of the development and functions of state social work and, in Chapter 5, to an assessment of the various approaches.

4 The Development and Functions of Social Work

Despite claims to be found in some histories of social work (Kuenstler, 1961; Bessell, 1970), social work as we know it mounts no challenge to prostitution as the oldest servicing profession. Goetschius (in Kuenstler, 1961) may see concern for social welfare needs in the Buddhist, Egyptian and Jewish Scriptures. Bessell may discern startling similarities between the training of first-century Christian deacons and modern social work education. Social work, however, has much more recent origins, and state provision of personal social services is a veritable infant.

This chapter starts by tracing the roots of state social work and then proceeds to outline a range of understandings of the development and functions of that work.

Social Work Before the Welfare State

Most commentators on the history of social work trace its origins back to the middle of the nineteenth century. Some appear to see a positive and unilinear progression from the tradition of Victorian philanthropy through to the co-ordinated state provision of social work services in the twentieth century (Woodroofe, 1971). The ideology of the Poor Law (itself of much earlier origin) which marked the provision of help in the nineteenth century – dividing the poor into deserving, and therefore worthy of philanthropic action and undeserving to be punished for their feckless behaviour – is seen by some as also permeating the attitudes and activities of twentieth-century state welfare agencies (George, 1973).

Others have argued that social work as a discrete activity grew out of the failure of philanthropy. Philanthropic action, often administered by the same people who administered the Poor Law, had failed to eradicate social needs, and this failure was seen in the late nineteenth century as a blow to national prestige (Seed, 1973). As a result, 'social work came into being closely related to a need to repair the national image which had been spoilt by a dramatic exposure of social need and the failure of philanthropy' (Seed, 1973, p. 9).

Some recent commentators have seen the growth of private charity organizations like the Charity Organization Society in a different light. Parry and Parry identify the evangelical Christian revival of the mid nineteenth century as the seed bed from which social work grew and flourished (Parry, Rustin and Satyamurti, 1979). Evangelical Christianity, with its emphasis on personal salvation, is seen as having spawned a social work with an emphasis on rescuing the immoral or preventing immorality. The first sign of modern social work appeared during the 1850s with the introduction of paid welfare workers associated with the Church and directed mainly at the moral welfare of women and girls (Walton, 1975, p. 41).

Others see the origins of modern social work as rooted in quite a different morality. For Steadman Jones (1971) the roots of nineteenth-century philanthropic and social welfare action are better seen in the need for a well-socialized proletariat in order to integrate all sections of the population into the structure, culture, norms and values of capitalist society and prevent social revolution. He reminds his readers of the philanthropist Samuel Smith's caution that

> I am deeply convinced that the time is approaching when this seething mass of human misery will shake the social fabric, unless we grapple more earnestly with it than we have done. . . . The proletariat may strangle us unless we teach it the same virtues which have elevated the other classes of society. (Steadman Jones, 1971, p. 291)

No doubt the ideologies of nationalism, evangelical Christianity, capitalist self-interest and secular philanthropy overlapped and interacted in the early development of social work as they, no doubt, also did in the development of the settlement movement in the late nineteenth century.

Settlements, often attached to universities, and in some ways the forerunners of community development activities (Seed, 1973), were established with the stated intention of providing educational and recreational facilities for the inhabitants of poor city areas (Woodroofe, 1971, pp. 56–76; Parry Rustin and Satyamurti, 1979, pp. 24–6).

Out of this hotchpotch of nineteenth-century social welfare activity developed, in the twentieth century, a series of systems of social welfare which were to exist until the late 1940s. Social work activities, which focussed particularly, though not exclusively, on the poor – as children, parents and elderly relations – were undertaken by a strong charity sector and a variety of central and local government departments (Woodroofe, 1971, pp. 193–8).

Coverage of need was patchy and the activities of different agencies were largely uncoordinated. It was not until the late 1940s that the state started to develop comprehensive social welfare services as part of a wider welfare state package.

One of the crucial tasks of this chapter is to provide a range of ways of understanding why and to what effect during the late twentieth century the state has intervened more comprehensively in personal social service provision.

The Inception of State Social Work

Following the Second World War, and in part in response to the report of the Curtis Committee (Curtis, 1946), three state social work agencies were created. These agencies, located at the level of the local state, replaced in large part the multiplicity of independent and government agencies which had previously carried out personal social service functions. These three social welfare agencies, which existed until the early 1970s and were primarily concerned with services to children, the physically and mentally sick and disabled and the elderly, carried out a range of mostly statutory responsibilities. These were especially concerned with the provision of residential or substitute care for clients in situations where home based care was regarded as inappropriate, inadequate or damaging (see Sainsbury, 1977, for a fuller description of the services).

The Reorganization of State Social Work

In the early 1970s, following the report of the Seebohm Committee (Seebohm, 1968) in 1968 and the passing of the Local Authority Social Services Act in 1970, state social work was reorganized into unified local authority departments charged with the provision of statutory and non-statutory services to those in need. This pattern of organization still pertains. In the following sections of the chapter we will be seeking to understand these organizational as well other practice related developments in state social work over the last forty years.

The Development and Functions of State Social Work

Reformist views

It will come as no surprise that implicit in many reformist views of the initial and later development of state social work services are ides about the growth of a collective conscience in modern British society. Sometimes such views are made explicit.

Slack, commenting on the introduction of state social work with children, says of the Curtis Report, '[it] was based on a *new and more sympathetic* approach to human need. Emphasis was laid on the differences of each child and his value as an individual' (Slack, 1966, p. 111, my emphasis).

Hall is similarly convinced that social service provision by the state is rooted in a fuller recognition of common humanity. Further, social service is 'essentially the manifestation of a personal interest in a human situation, a recognition of the uniqueness and value of the individual and of *our common humanity*' (Hall, 1952, p. 3, my emphasis).

The initial development of state social work should be seen, as far as the explicit social conscience writers are concerned, as the culmination of a process of growth in understanding and concern. It should be regarded as reflecting society's new commitment to meet need through the activities of government and state: 'whenever or wherever a social service is introduced it is to meet a need that has, whether soon or late, been recognised as real or unmet' (Slack, 1966, p. 93).

The initial development of large scale state social work has to be seen, for these writers, within a concept of social policy development, economically summarized by Titmuss: 'As the accepted area of social obligation widened, as injustice became less tolerable, new services were separately organised around individual need' (Titmuss, 1963, p. 21).

The initial involvement of the state in social work on a large scale is thus conceived by social conscience reformist writers as simply another manifestation of the growth of social conscience in society, of a developing rational and informed consensus. Once need is identified then society, through the state, intervenes in appropriate and moral ways to meet that need.

Similar social conscience formulations can be found in the literature to explain later developments both in legislation associated with social work and in the organizational context of state social work. Some authors implicitly accept a social conscience thesis of social policy development in their understandings of the development of, for example, social legislation concerned with children and young people (Sainsbury, 1977, part 1; Jones, 1971; 1981).

A common theme in such literature is that the Children and Young Persons' Acts of 1963 and 1969 should be located within a model of social policy development which emphasizes the idea of the perfectability of humankind. These, and other pieces of social legislation, should therefore be regarded as having developed out of 'a widening and deepening knowledge of need' (Barker, 1979, p. 178) and to be part of a continuous and cumulative process evolving 'constantly . . . in the direction of greater generosity and wider range' (Barker, 1979, p. 178).

Specifically, the 1963 Act, which sanctioned preventive social work to combat the need to receive troubled or troublesome children into local authority care, and the 1969 Act, which laid down a framework intended to minimize the number of child and young adult offenders appearing before courts – and saw a treatment or welfare model as more appropriate than a justice model in such cases – are seen as manifestations of the informed reactions of a benevolent state.

Social workers and others, it is argued, had in the post-war years become increasingly convinced that the causes of many problems associated with childhood were of a social or familial nature rather than of an individual nature. Consequently, it was suggested that problems of children's relationships with their parents or siblings were best dealt with within the family setting. Similarly, problems of juvenile criminality, associated with causative factors wider than the individual, were more justifiably dealt with by welfare intervention than by punishment.

Such legislation and the social work practice implied by it, should therefore be seen as humane societal responses, through the state, to greater knowledge about the causes of difficulties. Evidence had been produced of a wider network of factors associated with such problems than had previously been accepted. That evidence had prompted a number of further investigations by the state and by political parties (Longford, 1966; Home Office, 1965; 1968) and had eventuated in rational and moral responses in the form of social legislation and social work practices to cater for a minority of people experiencing difficulties.

The reorganization of local authority social services in the early 1970s is explained in this perspective in similarly unproblematic terms. The social conscience literature again highlights two key factors as explaining this organizational change: improved knowledge and greater benevolence. In the twenty years following the inception of a state controlled social service system, knowledge of two kinds was amassed by practitioners and administrators in the services. Firstly it came to be generally accepted that the tripartite organizational form of state services led to both duplication of tasks and uneven coverage of need (Seebohm, 1968). Secondly, as we have already noted, 'knowledge' was being generated that the causes of need for a minority of the population were wider and more complicated than had previously been thought and might be affected by structural and societal factors over which the individual had little control (Townsend and Abel Smith, 1965; Longford, 1966). As a consequence, practitioners, academics and sympathetic politicians called for a unified service which would theorize and meet the needs of the individual within the context of his relationship to family, community and society (Marshall, 1975, pp. 143–64). These calls, supplemented by the reports of various government committees, and particularly the Seebohm Report, eventuated in the reorganization of state social work.

Such views, of course, have much in common with Marshall/Crosland type formulations about the development of welfare in general and social work in particular. For 'Marshallites' the state provision of social work services must be seen, along with other welfare interventions, as a result of a societal consensus that the state should provide social rights to all its members. In pre-twentieth-century Britain, social work intervention had been available only to the poor and then in a stigmatizing form. The development of universal state personal social services in the postwar period had resulted from agreement on giving all sections of the population access to non-stigmatizing personal social services (Crosland, 1956; Marshall, 1963) and thereby to equality of status if not to economic equality.

For Crosland, and the strand of social democracy represented by his work, state co-ordinated social work services and their further development grew out of a desire to help the small residue of disadvantaged people in post-capitalist society (Crosland, 1956, pp. 81–101).

The development of state social work is, then, from a reformist position theorized within a wider context which presumes a transformation of societal attitudes (and of society itself) as a result of a growth in collective commitment to meet the needs of disadvantaged individuals or groups. That commitment is itself, in large part, the result of increases in knowledge and understanding. This being so, what might be the aims and functions of state social work as seen from this perspective?

AIMS AND FUNCTIONS OF STATE SOCIAL WORK

As we have seen from our consideration of the development of state social work, twentieth-century British society is regarded as having experienced a transformation from unbridled free market capitalism to a welfare state society. As a result of that transformation, and particularly as a result of welfare state policies, the extremes of primary deprivation had been eradicated. Only a minority of disadvantaged people, it was believed, still fell outside the advantages conferred by a transformed and welfare oriented post-capitalist society. Certainly, then, in the 1950s the aims and functions of social work were conceived by proponents of a reformist approach as the 'relief of residual distress' (Crosland, 1956, pp. 85–94). Though primary poverty was belived to have been eradicated by the welfare state, residual secondary poverty continued to exist alongside the problems of physical and mental illness and disability present in any society. The primary function of social work was therefore to be the amelioration of such conditions.

Some 1950s commentators make this more explicit. Penelope Hall, arguing that all major social problems had been successfully tackled by welfare state policies, proposed that the function of social work should therefore be to proceed to tackle more sophisticated problems.

> The most urgent problems . . . today are such symptoms of a sick society as the increasing number of marriage breakdowns, the spread of juvenile delinquency and the sense of frustration of the worker in spite of improved pay and conditions . . . that is, problems of maladjustment rather than material need. (Hall, 1952, p. 8)

If this conviction that primary need had been outlawed was shattered by the 'rediscovery of poverty' in the 1960s

(Townsend and Abel Smith, 1965), the basic reformist approach remained substantially unchanged. The functions of social work came to include helping government more fully to understand how pockets of deprivation and need remained in a postwar society characterized by rising living standards and relative affluence (Jenkins, 1972; Joseph, 1972). Poverty and need along with a catalogue of other problems were increasingly regarded as being outside the control of the individual (see pp. 63–76). However, a fundamental basis of reformism was that society had been transformed. Problems of deprivation and need were therefore hypothesized as having roots in institutions intermediate to the individual and society. Thus the aims of social work in Seebohm departments were to include the articulation and treatment of individual problems in the context of family and community (Seebohm, 1968). These aims were also to be met by state sponsored community development projects (in the early 1970s) seemingly established to research and then change communities and thus ameliorate or eradicate need amongst marginal populations (Loney, 1983).

Reformist approaches to social work, then, have presented the functions of social work as the relief of residual distress, the amelioration of need and the harmonizing of malfunctioning societal subsystems with the major society. Such functions, it has been believed, would fulfil Crosland's conviction that the state should provide a welfare minimum (Crosland, 1956) and would also constitute steps on the road to the eradication of preventable social need.

Industrial State Theories and Social Work

THE DEVELOPMENT OF SOCIAL WORK

According to this approach the provision of state co-ordinated social work services has been determined by the logic of industrialism. Early and later industrialization had, as we have seen earlier, the effect of separating industrial workers and their families from previously experienced informal networks of emotional and material support. Consequently the informal networks of support were progressively replaced by more formal and, ultimately, state controlled personal social services systems called forth by actual or potential social fragmentation (see Mishra, 1981, pp. 39–44 for a summary of these arguments).

The American writers Wilensky and Lebaux (1965), underline the dramatic effects that industrialization had on the social structure and the fabric of individual and family lives. The stresses of industrialization have been reflected in developed industrial nations in rising rates of divorce, delinquency and other social problems. Such problems are seen as, in large part, resulting from the fracturing of the individual's relationships with informal and close networks of support.

Such problems also represent, along with labour protest at the impact of industrialization, the engine of social reform driving industrial states to the provision of welfare. State social work (as well as other welfare interventions) were therefore developed. That they were necessary was the result of industrialization. That state expenditure was available to fund state social work was similarly dependent on a process of profitable industrialization.

AIMS AND FUNCTIONS OF SOCIAL WORK

From this perspective the aims and functions of state social work can be stated quite simply. They are twofold and relate to system integration and social integration.

State social work may be seen as contributing to system integration in the following ways. Industrial development depends on societal subsystems being integrated around the core societal prerequisite of developing industry. In order to achieve that integration industrial states must intervene through social and economic policy to provide the economic conditions and the appropriate labour force for successful development. As we have seen (Chapter 3), the economic conditions for successful development are aided by state intervention to provide income maintenance systems. A productive workforce is enhanced by the provision of state health care systems. Education policies may aid the development of an appropriately skilled labour force. Social work may be seen as facilitating integration through its socialization functions. That is to say, social work may be seen, from this perspective, as primarily functioning, through its child care and delinquency related interventions, to ensure that the present and future workforce are appropriately socialized or resocialized into attitudes towards work which promote further and profitable industrial development.

State social work may also be seen as contributing to social integration. Conflicts or difficulties, arising in part from the stresses of industrial development, may on occasion threaten the cohesion of social institutions such as the family which play an important part in the reproduction of the labour force. Social work, in acting to prevent fractures in social institutions, contributes to social integration.

Marxist Views of Social Work

As might be expected, Marxist views on the development and functions of social work differ radically from both of the perspectives so far considered in this chapter. As we might expect, there are also sharp differences of emphasis within the overall Marxist perspective on social work.

THE DEVELOPMENT OF STATE SOCIAL WORK

For many Marxists, one of the keys to understanding the later development of state social work is to be found in an understanding of the development of modern social work in the late nineteenth century.

Many Marxist historians of the period (Thompson, 1963; Hobsbawm, 1964; Harrison, 1965; Williams, 1968; Steadman Jones, 1971) draw attention to two important political characteristics of urban British life in the late nineteenth century. First, it is argued, this period saw growing political disaffection among the respectable working class. Secondly, it is contended, an underclass came to be perceived as a far greater threat to social stability than had hitherto been the case.

Housing shortages and poor housing and other intolerable social conditions are seen as having created circumstances in which the respectable working class became more receptive to radical political ideas (Williams, 1968; Steadman Jones, 1971). A worsening of such conditions had also further immiserated the residuum, that is the casual unemployed or lower working classes. In such conditions, the lower working classes posed a threat to social stability not only because 'crammed together in filthy, airless and noisy one room tenements, it was inevitable that the poor would be brutalised and sexually immoral . . . ' (Steadman Jones, 1971, p. 286). The existence of an immoral and brutalized sub working class posed other threats also. Its perpetuation would mean that generations of the poor would further degenerate morally, precipitating the risk of unruly and socially disruptive mob behaviour. The existence of such an alienated class of people living cheek by jowl with the respectable working class also posed the risk of political and physical contamination of higher social classes in society. Late-nineteenth-century London and other cities were therefore perceived as seething cauldrons of potential political unrest and social and physical disease.

These social and political realities are seen as having engendered a major change in middle class attitudes to the residuum. Fear of a radical working class and a socially contaminating residuum provoked an assault on unbridled *laissez-faire* politices from the political right as well as from the political left at that time.

It is in this context that Marxist social historians seek to understand the reorientation of previous attitudes to social work and welfare. In earlier decades the Charity Organization Society and similar organizations had functioned to dispense relief to the working poor. In the circumstances of the late nineteenth century, poor relief, such as that administered through the Mansion House Appeal Fund in London, was dispensed, as a palliative and ransom against social unrest, to the residuum as well as to the respectable working poor. Previously, charity had been dispensed by middle class agencies who perceived themselves as morally and intellectually suited to administer philanthropic aid to their lesser brethren. At the close of the nineteenth century attitudes among the middle class welfare intellectuals had changed. Aid offered to the poor to facilitate self-help but administered in paternalistic ways came to be seen by some as a process contributing but little to the social integration of the respectable working classes. Some had argued for a 'practicable socialism' (Barnett, 1896) in which the respectable would be both integrated into mainstream capitalist society through the satisfaction of their legitimate grievances and enlisted as allies to the middle class in the battle against the residuum. Many had become convinced that 'the main evil of our present system of aid to the poor is its failure to enlist the co-operation of the working classes themselves' (Pigou, 1925, quoted in Steadman Jones, 1971).

By the late nineteenth century, then, attitudes to charitable social work and welfare were subject to winds of change. Strategies had been developed which emphasized welfare's functions as the co-option of the upper working class into mainstream society and the coercion of the residuum.

Developments in social work at this time can therefore be seen as having roots in strategies designed to protect capitalist society from social instability and political unrest. These may be seen as having resulted in welfare strategies intended to fragment the working classes through the co-option of one section of the working classes and the further alienation of the other (see Steadman Jones, 1971, pp. 303–14, for a fuller summary of these arguments).

SOCIAL WORK AND THE WELFARE STATE

Such strategies for welfare and such attitudes to the residuum also marked thinking about the poor in the four pre-welfare state decades. Barnett's enforced labour colonies for the unemployable poor (see Steadman Jones, 1971; Seed, 1973) may have been replaced by the Social Darwinism of the early-century Fabians and others (Jones, 1983), but ideas about social policy interventions into the lives of the lower working classes still included the unmistakable intention of punitive coercion. The object of work with the unemployed poor was seen not as rehabilitation but as containment and eradication.

> In dealing with men and women of this character we cannot hope to accomplish individual radical cure, we must, as with the feeble-minded, organise the extinction of the tribe . . .

We must attain the same result by the longer and gentler system of perpetual segregation in detention colonies and with all the mitigations that are practicable. (Whetham, 1909)

Social reformers of the political left, as well as those of the political right, emphasized the need to control the reproductive behaviour of the unemployed poor. Certain state benefits were withheld from them while made available to the rest of the working class population (Jones, 1983).

The political and social climate immediately predating the Second World War was, then, still impregnated by an ideology of poverty dependent on notions of the individual and group pathology of the poor. Social work action was clearly located within such an ideology (Woodroofe, 1971). Its functions were seen as including the social integration of the respectable working classes and the social segregation and control of the residuum (Jones, 1983). It is generally accepted by Marxists, as by others, that, over the forty years of welfare state social work, social welfare ideology and the practice it sustains has shifted from an emphasis on containment to an emphasis on rehabilitation. The problem for Marxists is in understanding the roots of such development and the nature of such a change. Whereas system determinists (or Marxist functionalists) must theorize developments in state social work as rooted in capitalist needs, some Marxists see the initial and later developments in state social work as reflecting changes in the relationship between state and civil society. Those changes are seen as having been influenced by political struggle. Whilst Marxist functionalists see state social work functioning to oppress or incorporate the working class, some Marxists theorize a degree of autonomy for the state and state functionaries from the interests of a dominant class. Consequently, they are able to see welfare functions as operating in the tension between competing class or group interests. For them state social work functions within a 'dialectic of welfare'.

From a Marxist functionalist standpoint the development of state social work has to be seen as part of a 'capitalist fraud'. State social work, like other elements in a welfare state, must be seen as having developed in response to the economic and ideological needs of developed capitalism (see Bailey and Brake, in Bailey and Brake, 1975). State health and education provision has been developed as a result of the need for a healthy and appropriately educated pool of labour. State housing programmes were developed, in large part, to satisfy the needs of capitalist enterprise for workforces housed adequately and in the proximity of their work places. Income maintenance systems were called forth as a means of aiding stability of consumption. Similarly, state social work is seen as having developed as a response to the need for an appropriately socialized and compliant working class. In such political circumstances sections of the working class have been incorporated into support for the development of welfare services, including social work, seeing them as improvements in the rights of working class people (Pearce, 1973). Social work, like other forms of state welfare is, whilst apparently constituting a response to working class pressure, little more than a historically specific response by the state to the needs of capitalism. It is seen as having developed inevitably out of the logic of capitalism.

Other Marxists, stressing the contradictory nature of state welfare and the relative autonomy of the state, locate the development of the state welfare in the context of a quite different set of social and political processes. Jones (1983) sees the development of state social work as part of the development of a set of welfare institutions which was itself, according to another author, part of a wider 'social democratisation of society' (Jessop, in Scase, 1980). The 1945 Settlement, the mixed economy and the development of state welfare services are all manifestations of a changed atmosphere. Social democracy, envigorated by popular demand, had responded to that demand by widening the access of working people to a range of welfare services.

Corrigan (1977) sees the initial and later developments of state social welfare as, in part, a response to class struggle for greater welfare (see also Corrigan, 1979; Corrigan and Leonard, 1978). It is left to Wilson to remind us with acerbic directness that Corrigan's formulation is inadequate as an explanation of social work development:

> Social work . . . can in no sense be seen as the outcome of class struggle. There has never been any demand by working people for welfare to be administered in this way, and indeed there has been a traditional hostility in the working class to 'the welfare'. . . . (Wilson, in Brake and Bailey, 1980)

Nonetheless, social work development can be quite legitimately regarded from this perspective as having its roots in a changed political atmosphere and transformed state. That state and that atmosphere, created in large part through class struggle, may have responded to more direct demands for health, education and housing than for social work. Social work services administered largely by the state must be seen, however, as no less a manifestation of the spirit of 1945 than the other services.

AIMS AND FUNCTIONS OF SOCIAL WORK

From a Marxist functionalist standpoint the aims and functions of state social work are strikingly clear. State social work is intended to function, and indeed functions in practice, to reproduce the relationships of capitalism and to resolve the contradictions of capitalism in a way which promotes the interests of a dominant class.

The state, according to this perspective, safeguards the interests and development of capitalism. The British welfare state is therefore seen as functioning to promote capital accumulation (O'Connor, 1973), economic efficiency and social stability (Saville, 1957) and ideological conformity (Barratt-Brown, 1972).

The place of state social work in this scheme is that of a state institution functioning primarily, though not exclusively, to promote social stability and the conformity of working class people to ruling class ideology. These functions may be facilitated by means of social case work techniques ' . . . a pseudo-science – that blames individual inadequacies for poverty and so mystifies and diverts attention from the real causes' (Case Con, 1970). They may also be facilitated by other, and seemingly more progressive, forms of social work such as group work and community work. In this view, though, such forms of work serve simply to pathologize the group or the community rather than the individual. Social work, then, whether practised in the form of case work, group work or community work, functions socially to integrate, or socially control, working class people. Its aim is to promote social stability in capitalist society by changing people as individuals, groups or communities and, in so doing, to protect the social, economic and ideological hegemony of a ruling class. Marxist functionalists therefore might well agree with Corrigan that 'throughout the western world, states are characterised by one of the two major symbols of control in capitalist society; the tank or the community worker' (Corrigan, in Leonard, 1975, p. 25). However, they are unlikely to believe that, given these aims and functions, social work can ever struggle against them or function in other and contradictory ways. Social case work is conceived as coercive activity which defines socially caused problems as family or individual crises (see Wilson, in Cowley, *et al.*, 1977). Community work and group work are seen as ' . . . means by which society induces individuals and groups to modify their behaviour in the direction of certain cultural norms' (Gulbenkian Foundation, 1968, p. 84).

Some Marxist writers on social work, however, perceive the aims and functions of social work differently. For these writers, the state, though generally predisposed to promote the interests of a dominant social class, possesses and at times exhibits a limited autonomy from that class. More than this, state welfare institutions and welfare workers also possess a degree of autonomy from the state. Consequently both aims and functions of state social work may be significantly affected by the use to which such relative autonomy is put.

For many writers from this perspective (Corrigan and Leonard, 1978; Bolger *et al.*, 1981; Jones, 1983) the aims and functions of social work throughout the late twentieth century manifest a dialectic of welfare (Leonard, in Bean and MacPherson, 1983).

Although state social work services can clearly be seen to function to promote social stability and integration, economic

efficiency and growth – and therefore to reinforce and reproduce the social and economic relationships of capitalist
society – such an analysis is, at best, only half the story. Co-
ordinated state social work services were established and have
functioned for most of the period in what relative autonomists
conceive as a changed political atmosphere and structure. The
spirit of 1945 (Jones, 1983) has been sustained throughout
much of the recent period. Social work legislation and social
work practice during that period has reflected the clear influence
of the social democratization of state structures and social
values. State policies and social work practices, while stopping
far short of the provision of total welfare, have demonstrated a
tendency for state social provision progressively to meet some
of the social needs of ordinary people as well as being
concerned with containment and control (Gough, 1979;
Leonard, in Bean and MacPherson, 1983). From this perspective,
then, co-ordinated state social work has functioned at one and
the same time to effect the contradictory aims of meeting some
of the social needs of its clients while meeting the economic
and political 'needs' of a dominant class in capitalist society.

Within this changed political structure, the aims and
functions of state social work are seen as having changed
fundamentally if not completely. Prior to the development of a
social democratic welfare state, the objectives of social work
with the poor are seen as having been those of punishment and
containment (Seed, 1973; Leonard, in Bailey and Brake, 1975;
Jones, 1983). Welfare state social work, reflecting the social
democratization of state structures and social practices, is seen
as still concerned, in part, with social control. However, the
emphasis of practice and legislation is seen as having moved
from punishment to rehabilitation. Postwar social democratic
politics had provided 'the ideological climate for [the] more
liberal and humane welfare theories and practices to be
extended to the unorganised and impoverished dependent poor'
(Jones, 1983, p. 39). It is, of course, true that such changes in
practice and aims have represented little more, at times, than a
replacement of biological determinist theories of social problem
causation by a set of family pathology explanations. Nonetheless such a shift, though limited and still ideologically useful to

powerful societal interests, is seen as having effected a move towards understanding social problems within a wider social context than hitherto.

Policies and practices related to youthful delinquency and family problems can be seen, from this perspective, as reflecting the social democratic dialectic of welfare. The 1969 Children and Young Persons' Act might therefore be conceptualized as part of a process which highlights the tendency of social democratic thinking on welfare both to liberate and control.

The 1969 Act and the reorganization of personal social services, with which it was associated temporally and philosophically, point up both the progressive and conservative nature of state social work under social democracy. The Act and the reorganization are seen as products of the contradictions inherent in the capitalist system. For both sought to establish the primacy of a welfare model in the theory and practice of social work: the Act by elevating the welfare needs of young offenders above abstract considerations of justice in sentencing; reorganization by promoting the idea that the new social service departments would provide for the welfare needs of all in a non-stigmatizing way. At the same time, however, both social policy developments are seen as being rooted in an ideology of family pathology which saw residual problems in social democratic Britain as the result of malfunctioning family units. Such an ideology reinforced a new form of social control in social work. Individuals, previously held responsible for their own difficulties were, in late-twentieth-century British social democracy, to be subject to social control through treatment rather than punishment. They were to be controlled through the identification and policing of families – often seen as the root of problems of deviancy and poverty (see Donzelot, 1980).

For the relative autonomists, such considerations demonstrate crucial weaknesses in Marxist functionalist and reformist approaches. The first is that both approaches present views on the functions of social work which are inadequate because they ignore the real, if limited, gains and the equally real constraints for clients which the primacy of a welfare principle in personal social service work constitutes. Specifically such analyses ignore that state social work is a dynamic and contradictory state activity in which many of its methods and theories can be used along a wide continuum that has repressive objectives at one end and more liberal and humane possibilities at the other (Jones, 1983, pp. 40–1).

The second weakness relates to both reformist and Marxist functionalist analyses of class and state. Reformist formulations are seen as inadequate because they ignore the relationship between the ideas and actions of a dominant class and welfare policy. Consequently, reformist formulations regard clients as in some ways responsible for socially induced problems by theorizing the problem family as the source of difficulties in an otherwise harmonious post-capitalist society (Clarke, 1980). System determinist approaches to social work are similarly flawed. As Clarke reminds us,

> In analysing the capitalist state it is tempting to see it as a homogeneous bloc acting on behalf of capital against the working class. In fact what is revealed in the development of the 1969 Act is the complexity of its internal composition (Clarke, 1980, p. 94)

The contradictory nature of welfare aims and functions is also one of the main themes of a recent contribution to the literature on socialist social work (Bolger *et al.*, 1981).

The development, the aims and the functions of social work are seen as subject to a struggle of forces and ideas for which the state has been the arena. For them, the development and aims of social work can be seen as the result of a capitalist class's desire to reproduce the workforce. At the same time, they argue 'working people realised that there were forms of state intervention that would stop them dying or from leading such brutalised lives' (Bolger *et al.*, 1981, p. 21).

These authors, while acknowledging the limits of welfare in a capitalist society, also wish to argue for the reality of social work activity in social democracy as an activity with liberal and humane possibilities. Further, they see social work policy in this period as facilitating liberal and humane (albeit partial) welfare practice. Further developing Clarke's treatment of the

1969 Act in an earlier article (Clarke, in Parry, Rustin and Satyamurti, 1979), they argue as follows. First, they see the Act as riven with ideological contradictions of the nature outlined above. However and secondly, they argue, it represented an attempt by the state to come to some partial understanding of a different model of the causation of social behaviour than had hitherto been dominant (Bolger *et al.*, 1981, p. 91). While a justice model of punishment is quintessentially individualistic, its replacement by a welfare model marked progress.

> In any form of progress towards a socialist society it is essential to move from such ideology and practice. We see the welfare model as the first small step towards that objective . . . it needs to contain a different understanding of what causes criminal behaviour. But it does represent one of the few moves . . . away from individualism in causation. (Bolger *et al.*, 1981, p. 93)

Relative autonomy approaches to social work aims and functions, then, replace the simplicity of system determinism with the complexity of social and ideological struggle. Of course, analyses which posit a welfare dialectic have significant implications for the development of social work practice (see, for instance, Cohen, in Bailey and Brake, 1975; Leonard, in Bailey and Brake, 1975; Leonard, in Timms and Watson, 1976; Corrigan and Leonard, 1978; Wilson, in Brake and Bailey, 1980). These implications will be developed in a later chapter.

Feminist Views about Social Work

Part of the feminist critique of welfare (see Chapter 3) which has developed in recent years relates specifically to state social work. We therefore move to a review of feminist views on social work.

THE DEVELOPMENT OF STATE SOCIAL WORK

Feminist commentators on the development of co-ordinated state social work services, whether they draw on Marxist or reformist perspectives of the state, make a particular contribution to the understanding of social work development. Put simply, these commentators underline the importance of women in the development of social work from its nineteenth-century roots through to the dawning of the welfare state. The conditions associated with the early development of social work – philanthropic concern, fear of social revolution, dented national pride, etc. – led to the provision of voluntary services staffed largely by women. That social work activity was the activity of an elite is undisputed (Brook and Davis, 1985) but for much of the pre-welfare state period that elite was female. Middle and upper class women, often unmarried but sometimes the wives of the rich, were recruited into the ranks of a social work preoccupied with the rescue of widows, orphans, prostitutes and the poor in general. As a result a paradoxical situation often arose in which, according to Wilson,

> middle class women with no direct experience of marriage and motherhood themselves took on the social task of teaching marriage and motherhood to working class women who were widely believed to be ignorant and lacking when it came to their domestic tasks. (Wilson, 1977, p. 46)

This notwithstanding, social work in the late nineteenth and early twentieth centuries became largely the province of middle and upper class women (a process well documented by Timms, 1967, and Walton, 1975). Feminist writers (including Wilson, 1977; Brook and Davis, 1985) have also been instrumental in excavating from a largely male oriented history the reminder that, although such social work activity was predominantly the province of women, the management committees of the voluntary organizations which administered the activity were predominantly men. In this task they have been ably assisted by some male commentators (notably, Walton, 1975).

AIMS AND FUNCTIONS OF SOCIAL WORK

Much of the feminist analysis of social work's aims and functions draws attention to the relationship between the state and the family in capitalist (and other 'advanced') societies. For

Gieve, the welfare state in general and social work in particular 'highlights the link between the state and the family and the way in which the state systematically bolsters the dependent-woman family' (Gieve, in Allen, 1974). For Loney and collaborators, 'the welfare system as it stands (or totters) is utterly dependent upon a specific construction of gender' (Loney, Boswell and Clarke, 1984).

For most feminist writers, postwar welfare state social work, and particularly its family interventionist activities, reinforce women's unequal and oppressed position in capitalist society as well as reinforcing other dominant ideas. Pascall, echoing many other feminist writers, conceives of the modern family as a deeply ambiguous social formation (Pascall, in Bean and McPherson, 1983). Although the family may be seen as an arena where the values of caring and sharing are upheld, it is also the arena where women's dependency is nurtured. It therefore constitutes the focal point for exploitative relationships between men and women. According to many feminist writers, the welfare state, and social work in particular, functions to entrench, reinforce and reproduce women's dependency and exploitation in the family and thus to perpetuate fundamental inequalities between the sexes.

To appreciate the key concepts in a feminist understanding of the aims and functions of social work it is useful to reconstruct here the important steps in feminist arguments about welfare. One of the most influential of contemporary feminist writers on welfare has argued that the welfare state in general constitutes 'a set of ideas about the family and about women as the linch-pin of the family' (Wilson, 1977, p. 9). As such it also constitutes a mechanism by which women's traditional roles as wife and mother may be controlled (Wilson, 1977, p. 40). Social work, like the welfare state as a whole, performs functions which both protect the interests of a dominant social class and oppress or exploit women. It does so by the construction of an ideal type of family and by monitoring or policing families which fail to conform to this ideal type. Specifically, the dependent breadwinner form of family is theorized as functional for the reproduction of the labour force and thus capital (Wilson, 1980, p. 31; Althusser, 1971). It is also seen as necessary for creating the dependency behaviours and demands for gratification which are functional for the perpetuation of a hierarchical social and production system (Wilson, 1980, p. 31).

In contemporary capitalist society such family formations also imply the creation and sustenance of economic dependency for most women. Social work, it is argued, functions as one amongst many state institutions which play an important ideological role in perpetuating women's dependency and exploitation. It does so, according to Wilson, by seeking to reinforce the most conformist types of family patterns (Wilson, 1980, p. 32), often in the face of a surrounding society in which conventional family patterns are disintegrating.

How then, exactly, has social work carried out these functions? Feminist writers may point to a large number of developments in state social work to support a view that the aims and functions of social work are, and have been, deeply discriminatory or oppressive to women. Below we outline but a few examples from the theory and practice of social work:

(1) It has been argued, for instance, that the report of the Curtis Committee on Child Care (though chaired by a woman and having women as half its membership) reinforced an increasingly popular view, shared by Bowlby (1953) that the care of children was best carried out in families with non-working, dependent mothers. (Brook and Davis, 1985, p. 15)

(2) It is further argued that the dependant–breadwinner form of family organization was reinforced by the subcommittee of the women's group on Public Welfare in 1948 which argued 'Frequently a family can survive in spite of a weak or vicious father but it is rare that it can survive with an incapable mother' (Women's Group, 1948, quoted in Brook and Davis, 1985).

(3) Social work, it is argued, has imbibed an ideology of maternal care (see Ehrenreich and English, 1979) which, in practice, has restricted women's capacity to act with approval in any other role than that of dependent wife and mother. To this end social work's concern in the 1950s

and 1960s with latch-key children placed working class women especially in an impossible double-bind. If such women did not work their families were often driven into poverty. If they did, they ran the risk of being labelled by social work agencies as neglectful mothers (Brook and Davis, 1985, p. 16). Competent parenting, it is contended from this perspective, is interpreted in social work theory and practice as competent mothering. Competent mothering implies the absence of paid work outside the home and thus economic dependency on a man, preferably in a state sanctioned dependant–breadwinner family.

(4) Similarly, it is argued, problems of delinquency and maladjustment are often, implicitly or explicitly, conceptualized in social work as problems of malfunctioning families and often as problems arising from absent, working, mothers (Comer, 1971), or as a result of child-rearing occurring outside the safe confines of the dependant–breadwinner nuclear family. Specifically, it is argued by some feminists, social work constructs a model of successful child development which implies the necessity of a 'normal' family context. Moreover, the creation of such a context is seen as depending on the competence (and perhaps full time presence) of the mother (McIntosh, in McLennan, Held and Hall, 1984, pp. 228–9).

(5) Finally, it is argued, state policies encouraging, whilst underfinancing, community care of the old or sick, and social work practices rooted in the concept of partnership with carers further reinforce traditional family patterns and, in consequence, women's oppression/exploitation as carers (see Finch and Groves, 1983; McIntosh, in McLennan, Held and Hall, 1984; Brook and Davis, 1985).

What emerges then from this rather thematic reconstruction of feminist arguments about social work is a view that the aims and functions of social work include the crucial aims of:

(1) reinforcing through theory and practice an ideology of the family rooted in a dependant–breadwinner form of family structure;

(2)   policing families (see Donzelot, 1980; Meyer, 1983),
      especially those who fail to conform to such patterns;
(3)   entrenching, reinforcing and reproducing the dis-
      crimination, exploitation and oppression of women in
      contemporary society.

The 'Radical Right' and Social Work

As we have seen in Chapter 3, radical right formulations see
social welfare as having developed as the result of the creation
of a bogus consensus on the need for state provision. Many, if
not all, of the arguments adduced by proponents of anti-
collectivism in relation to welfare in general can be adduced in
the specific case of social work provision. What concerns us
here is to outline some important historical and contemporary
concerns of the radical right about state social work.

   For the radical right state provision of social work, like other
state social services, has led British society towards state
coercion (Hayek, 1944, p. 52; Friedman, 1962, p. 13). Social
work, by according citizen rights to all sections of the
population, is also conceived of as having contributed to social
discord (Friedman, 1962, ch. 10) and, because of its increasing
call on the public purse, to reduce economic growth in
prosperity. State social work can also be seen, from this
perspective, as having contributed to a diminution of individual
responsibility in the population at large because it, along with
other social policies, 'reduces the breadwinner's individual
responsibility for his family's well being, and for the pursuit of
independence it substitutes permanent mutual dependence as
the much more fragile basis of mutual respect' (Bremner, 1968,
pp. 52–3).

   Inasmuch as the state provision of social work services has
superseded the workings of the capitalist market-place, 'the
voluntary co-operation of individuals' (Friedman, 1962, p. 13),
it has functioned to reduce freedom: it has also had the effect of
reducing democracy, choice, respect, the role of the family and
has contributed to social disorganization and sluggish economic
growth.

   The new conservative apologists of the postwar years have

therefore prescribed a much reduced role for state social work in contemporary British society. Instead of state social work offering a more or less universal service, social welfare services are seen as best undertaken in the main by the family and the community. Thatcher, echoing Friedman, has argued that 'if we are to sustain, let alone extend, the level and standard of care in the community, we must first try to put responsibility back where it belongs, with the family and with the people themselves' (Thatcher, 1977, p. 83).

Such a pre-eminent role for voluntary, family, or community services, and a consequential residual role for state social work, is also clear in the statements of Thatcher government ministers. Jenkin, then Secretary of State for Social Services, argued in 1981 that 'The Social Services departments should seek to meet directly only those needs which others cannot or will not meet . . . Their task is to act as a safety net . . . for people for whom there is no other, not a first port of call' (Guardian, 21 January, 1981).

Thatcher herself told the 1981 annual conference of the Women's Royal Voluntary Service that the main burden of social welfare provision should fall on the voluntary sector of welfare, with statutory social services functioning simply as residual gap fillers, underpinning the work of the voluntary sector.

Notwithstanding such prescriptions and the current emphasis on community care and partnership schemes, reports of state social work's imminent death seem exaggerated. We have dealt in Chapter 1 with explanations of why the policy prescriptions of the new conservatives have not fully materialized in seven years of Thatcher government. We turn in the next chapter to an assessment of explanations of the relationship between the state and welfare. That chapter will seek to construct what the author regards as the most plausible account of welfare development and functions and will act as a springboard from which both further to analyse contemporary developments in welfare and to prescribe directions in which reflective and critical practice in welfare might be possible and effective.

5 *State, Welfare and Social Work*

In the earlier chapters of this book the reader has been confronted by a range of possible understandings of the development and functions of state intervention in modern Britain. Specific efforts have been made to demonstrate how various theories or perspectives seek to explain increased state involvement of one sort or another in civil society in the period since 1945. Consideration has been given to the ways in which various theories of the state and society are reflected in the social welfare literature, and particularly in that literature which focusses on the development and functions of welfare state policies. In the last chapter our attention was further focussed as we were confronted with a range of understandings of state social work policy.

The remaining chapters of this book will build on this descriptive and historical base in order to provide a critical analysis of both social welfare theory and social welfare practice. In particular, this chapter and the next will attempt to tackle two major tasks:

(1) a critical analysis of the various perspectives described in Chapters 2–4 in order to provide both a plausible under-standing of the history of state welfare and a theoretical framework within which to understand the problems and possibilities of state social work;

(2) the development of that critical analysis in order to show how such a 'sociological imagination' (Mills, 1959) is potentially invaluable in informing a critical and reflective social work practice as well as in understanding contem-porary and historical systems of welfare.

Theories of State Welfare: Critique and Assessment

On first encounter, some or all of the perspectives considered in earlier chapters may seem equally plausible accounts of the development and functions of state intervention in the economy and welfare. The sociological enterprise to be undertaken in this chapter is, quite simply, to offer an assessment of which perspective or perspectives provide the most plausible account of recent state interventionism. In such an enterprise we cannot hope to do more than construct a plausible sociological account grounded in the empirical realities of state policy and practice. The searcher after abstract truth is therefore doomed to disappointment. What follows is what appears to the author to constitute the most plausible, the most adequate account of the social reality of welfare. Its adequacy as a sociological explanation must be judged on the basis of its social utility: does it provide the reader with the most convincing account of the development and functions of state welfare in general and state social work in particular?

State, Welfare and Reformist Views

Readers will remember that reformist perspectives on state and welfare are based on a number of core assumptions: about the nature of society; about the relationship of the state to government on the one hand and society on the other; about the social forces associated with large scale interventionism including welfare development; and about the functions of state welfare.

The question that concerns us here is a straightforward one. How adequate an account of the nature of society, state and welfare and of the development of state interventionism in civil society does this perspective provide?

The reformist perspective certainly appears to have two particular strengths. In the first place, unlike the industrial state perspective and the radical right viewpoint, it has a quite explicit theory of the relationship between the various social institutions which make up the contemporary British social structure. That is to say, it roots its hypotheses about state, society and welfare in a clearly enunciated interpretation of political structure. Another undoubted strength is that its claims and interpretations are clearly located in discussions of concrete social phenomena (e.g. Crosland's discussion of the dispersal of ownership of the means of control, in Crosland, 1952, or Marshall's discussion of the historical development of citizen rights, in Marshall, 1963) rather than being carried out at the level of abstract theory. It may be, however, that its strengths as an explanatory perspective are outweighed by a multiplicity of apparent weaknesses.

In the first place, it arguably overstates the scope of societal consensus over social values and social actions even at the inception of the period of mixed economy and social welfare. So that, for example, Marshall (1963, p. 110) appears to imply clearly that the introduction of compulsory tripartite secondary education in the 1940s reflected a consensus on the goal of providing a complete package of social rights to all citizens. Other authors (Rubinstein and Simon, 1973; Fenwick, 1976; Reynolds and Sullivan, 1986) clearly outline the degree of dissension over the question and the form of compulsory secondary education at this time.

Secondly, even if we accept reformism's theory of liberal democracy, its claim that major government policies are likely to reflect societal consensus over social values and social actions is at least suspect. It is, of course, true that examples of policy-making can be found which would appear to support this contention. The reorganization of secondary schooling in the 1960s – a major piece of educational policy-making – certainly reflected the aspirations of a wide cross-section of the British population (Benn and Simon, 1972; Rubinstein and Simon, 1973; Fenwick, 1976; Reynolds and Sullivan, 1986). It is, however, also true that examples of policy-making can be found throughout the postwar period which appear to demonstrate that government policy is as likely to run counter to public opinion as to reflect dominant trends in it. The decision by government in the late 1940s to proceed with development of the A-bomb appears, at least on the surface, to have flown in the face of a general public sympathetic to Britain's wartime ally, the Soviet Union. Policies, in the 1980s, of restructuring state intervention and cutting the welfare state appear to run counter to public opinion when it has been sampled (see Taylor-Gooby, 1985).

Perhaps one of the most contentious propositions contained within the reformist perspective, however, is the presentation of the state as the handmaiden of government. The state, it is argued, is a set of politically impartial social institutions. Government determines policy: state institutions merely execute policy. A brief glimpse at some examples of the relationship between state and government in the postwar period may suffice to make us profoundly suspicious of such a proposition.

The circumstances surrounding the establishment of the Department of Economic Affairs as a new government department in 1964 provides one such example. It was clear from the 1964 election manifesto (Labour Party, 1964) that, should the Labour Party, under Harold Wilson, form the government, it was intended to establish a new economic ministry to oversee and facilitate the reorganization of British industry (see pp. 11–12). That new ministry, the Department of Economic Affairs, would operate alongside and take over some of the responsibilities hitherto carried out by the Treasury. It is well documented (see, for example, Crossman, 1975; Crosland, 1982) that the Treasury civil service acted, at least initially, to thwart the work of the new department irrespective of the new government's wishes. If we are to believe the political diarists of the time, the established senior civil service resisted change by means which included the withholding of information from ministers. Examples of similar attempts to withhold information from government ministers, thereby curtailing policy options, and of attempts to impose the policy of the departmental civil service on ministers are documented by Crossman (1975, pp. 168–9) in relation to his tenure as Minister of Housing (1964–6). Other means by which the civil service directly influenced policy-making included the development of a civil service policy line presented with unanimity at cabinet committee meetings (Crossman, 1975, p. 198).

There are also examples, culled from the literature, of the civil service arm of the state acting consciously and in direct contravention of government policy. During the economic crisis of 1976 which led the British government to seek loan facilities from the IMF, Cabinet had decided at one point to refuse the conditions of the loan despite contrary advice from the Chancellor of the Exchequer. Notwithstanding this, Treasury officials are reported to have been negotiating the terms of a conditional loan within hours (Crosland, 1982, p. 378). Finally, an earlier example of policy-making and of the relationship between state and government throws further doubt on the validity of the reformist proposition. This example, relating to the reorganization of secondary schooling in the mid 1960s, quite clearly suggests that the civil service at times acts as a direct rather than an indirect policy-making body. In 1965 the Department of Education issued a circular (Circular 10/65) to local authorities requesting them to submit plans for the reorganization of their secondary school systems into comprehensive systems (see Benn and Simon, 1972; Rubinstein and Simon, 1973; Fenwick, 1976). It is now widely acknowledged that both the form of policy-making (circular rather than legislation) and the permissive nature of the circular (encouragement to reorganize rather than compulsion, the acceptance of a wide variety of comprehensive patterns of education, etc.) were the result of its drafting by civil service officials rather than politicians. In this case the influence of the civil service may, indeed, be seen to have been significant in that it contributed in no small way to the failure to develop in Britain a uniform system of comprehensive education to meet educational and social needs (Reynolds and Sullivan, 1986).

The proposition that the state occupies a handmaiden role to government is, then, thrown into some doubt by a consideration of the relationship in recent times between government and civil service.

Another problem with the reformist perspective on state and welfare is that it considerably under-theorizes the place of class or social group conflict/pressure in the development of state welfare services. It is, of course, true that Marshall (1963) draws attention to the role of conflict in forging a new consensus in British society over civil, political and social rights. It is equally true that Crosland (1952) perceives the growth of the labour movement as one of the factors associated with the transformation of capitalism. What we might later regard as a crucial weakness in the perspective, however, is its failure to theorize the relationship between opposing social forces as dynamic rather than static. Such dialectical changes may at times lead to apparent retreats from state welfare, at other times to increased involvement – a phenomenon which reformism has difficulty in explaining.

Further weaknesses are uncovered when we scrutinize the reformist literature on state intervention in general and the welfare state in particular. The idea that state intervention in welfare was intervention of a residual nature which would underwrite equality of opportunity in post-capitalist society (Crosland, 1952, 1956; Hall, 1952; Marshall, 1963; Slack, 1966) was, as we have seen, based on a number of claims. Key among them was the claim that British society had been transformed during the twentieth century from a capitalist to a post-capitalist society. Ownership had been dispersed, the power of labour had become a countervailing force to the power of capital. Equality of opportunity, partial until the mid twentieth century, had become a near reality through the development of a welfare state.

Empirical and other studies over the last quarter of a century have, however, attacked the foundations of the reformist edifice. Studies of poverty and inequality in the 1960s (Townsend and Abel-Smith, 1965) demonstrated the persistence of a substantial incidence of primary poverty in British society and, despite its relative lack of penetration into Tory or Labour ideology, dented the image of poverty as the experience of an inadequate minority.

Additionally, the pattern of ownership in British society and the social values of political elites appear to have remained unchanged in the postwar period (Blackburn, 1972). The increase in labour power which was undoubtedly a feature of the early postwar period has without doubt been severely curtailed by legislation and the state management of industrial relations and industrial disputes in the last ten years. Equality of access and opportunity, one of the pillars of reformist theories of state welfare aims and functions, has been shown to be a mirage. Inequality in educational opportunity has been demonstrated to have persisted throughout the postwar period (Halsey, Heath and Ridge, 1980). Equality of access to health care appears to have been a persistent myth (Tudor Hart, in Cox and Mead, 1975; Townsend and Davidson, 1982; Doyal, 1983). Equality of access to the personal social services has similarly failed to materialize. Indeed, evidence abounds which suggests that the welfare state, inasmuch as it has redistributed resources and life chances, has done so horizontally rather than vertically and has often benefited the rich rather than the poor (LeGrand, 1982; George and Wilding, 1984).

One final and significant weakness in the reformist perspective on state and welfare remains. As we have seen in a previous chapter, it presents us with considerable difficulties in theorizing the present state of welfare – be it crisis or not. If the state provision of welfare has developed, in part, as a result of the growth in collective conscience, how do we conceptualize cuts in social expenditure which have occurred consistently over at least the last decade? If society was truly transformed in the mid twentieth century, how have apparently defunct social and political values reappeared to guide the actions of state and government? As we have seen in previous chapters, one way out of this theoretical impasse may be to posit the existence of a further and retrogressive transformation in ideas about the state and state activities. Such a proposition, however, does pose further difficulties with and for the classic reformist position. Whilst it may be consistent to argue, within a perspective which upholds ideas as one of the most potent social influences on action, that changes in state welfare provision may reflect a new social consensus, much of the reformist literature on welfare is demonstrated to be intellectually flawed by such a theoretical sleight of hand. We may be able to explain the reversal of key elements of social welfare provision (e.g. the 1966 earnings related unemployment benefit, removed in 1982; the planned removal of fundamental benefits from the State Earnings Related Pension Supplement; the continuing process of partial closure of access to higher education) in terms of an adapted reformist position. Such an apparent retreat from welfare is, however, totally inexplicable in classic reformist approaches.

Reformist writers on welfare have constructed a model of state social welfare which is rooted in social democratic political philosophy and suggests that social policies are inherently benevolent as well as irreversible (Slack, 1966, p. 40; Robson, 1976, p. 34). To sustain such a model requires of us a refusal to evaluate not only the evidence of history but also the contemporary experience of state activities in welfare.

The reformist perspective, then, is seriously flawed. In consequence, students and practitioners might suspect that a critical sociological imagination will reveal difficulties of similar scope in the reformist view of social work. Certainly reformist nostrums about social work (see Chapter 4), which arguably constitute the commonsense understandings of social work, raise problems for the critical analyst. A view of the development of social work policy, whether related to child care, criminal justice, or organizational context, located so strongly in a model relying on ideas of changed morality, rationality of state response and fundamental changes in society, is certainly open to question. Similarly, the essentially integrative social work aims and functions theorized in the reformist approach appear to promote the interests of clients only if reformism's characterization of postwar British society as substantially just and socially conscious can be supported by sound evidence. Such evidence appears conspicuous by its absence.

Welfare, the Industrial State and Social Work

It has been suggested in earlier chapters that the important features of the 'industrial state and welfare' approach are twofold. They are:

(1) that systems of state welfare have developed in 'advanced' industrial nations in order to promote the interests and

satisfy the needs of industry for stable markets and appropriately educated, housed and healthy workforces;

(2) that the aims and functions of state welfare are those concerned with the integration of other societal subsystems around the core prerequisite of industrial development and the integration or reintegration of individuals into societal subsystems.

Unlike some approaches to the state and welfare it is possessed of one particular strength. It appears to be capable of explaining the development of any individual social policy intervention in its own right. Income maintenance policies developed in the early twentieth century and in the 1940s contributed to stability of demand for the products of corporate industrial enterprises. Educational innovations, such as the 1944 Act and the reorganization of secondary education in the 1960s, were responses to the demands of a technologically advancing industrial system for appropriately trained and educated personnel. Personal social service provision was developed as a result of geographical and social dislocation caused by the geographical mobility of workers in the early period of industrial development and in the early decades of this century. From this perspective most, if not all, social policies quite clearly serve the purpose of system integration, or social integration, or both. Income maintenance and education provision is seen as contributing to the integration of certain social subsystems, in this case public expenditure and schooling, into the drive for industrial development and stability. Personal social service systems, replacing the informal social care systems of family, community and church are seen as socially integrating potentially alienated or anomic individuals into the major social system.

Despite its apparent strength, in terms of grounding its explanations in concrete developments in the social structure of recent British society, this approach also has quite fundamental weaknesses.

In the first place, like most functionalist accounts, it is stronger at the level of description than it is at the level of analysis. It is certainly the case that almost all developed

industrial nations have welfare states. It may well be true that
the outcome of welfare policy has been to contribute to social
and system integration and to promote the interests of
corporate industry. To say this, however, is not necessarily the
same as saying that the industrial logic (Kerr *et al.*, 1962) is the
motive force for welfare state development or that the intention
of the state in developing welfare is largely or wholly to
promote the interests of industrial development. Functionalism
in general and the industrial state approach in particular tends
to see intention and outcome as necessarily directly related (see
Goldthorpe, 1962).

This approach to welfare development and function, it may
be thought, creates more problems than it resolves. It posits
welfare development as a response by the state to the needs of
industry. At no point does it address such questions as: 'how is
such need established?'; or 'who or what establishes that
particular needs exist?'. While appearing to present an analysis
of a dynamic process of welfare development this approach in
fact presents us with a puppet theatre model of development
and change. Developments in welfare are seen as responses to a
hidden motive force, that of the logic of industrialism. At no
time is this logic presented for analytic scrutiny. Instead we are
asked to deduce from the existence of state welfare systems in
industrial societies (the puppets) the existence of a prime mover
or puppeteer (the logic of industrialism).

Another difficulty with this approach is that a sort of societal
homeostasis appears to be implicit in its explanation of both
welfare development and function. The logic of industrialism
submerges the forces of diversity in society (ideology, social
class differences, race, religion, gender) and, consequently, acts
on and in a social structure dominated by the need and
inevitability of industrial development. As a result there is no
place in such an approach for considerations about how social
conflict between different social groups, classes, races or
genders may also form part of the motive force behind welfare
development, or part of the agenda of welfare functions.

The approach is, or appears to be, shot through with a
determinism which presents a picture of ultimate consensus on
the functional necessity of welfare systems to develop and

function in the service of an industrial logic which is, itself, extremely difficult to demonstrate (Goldthorpe, 1962). There is no place in this perspective for an analysis of the role of social group conflict or difference in the development and functions of welfare.

Finally this approach also presents us with some difficulties in theorizing the reorganization of state activities which appear to have occurred over the last decade. As noted in earlier chapters it might be adapted to demonstrate that, in a period of deindustrialization, the industrial logic argument works in reverse (if industry is contracting then there is less functional necessity for welfare support systems and more functional necessity for overt social control systems). As an explanatory model it is, however, almost entirely incapable of resolving an internal contradiction in its analysis. Galbraith (1972) supports an industrial logic argument by positing the interpenetration of state and industry in industrial societies so that the state, it is argued, has become an arm of corporate industry and corporate industry an arm of the state. If this contention were to be supported and the analysis sustained one would have expected resistance by the contemporary British state to the removal of subsidies to industry and the fairly rapid deindustrialization in many sectors of the manufacturing economy. Instead the state appears to have acted, through its interventions in the economy, to favour finance capital rather than industrial capital.

On close scrutiny the industrial state approach appears to be a deeply flawed model for understanding state activity in British society.

Its apparent analytic strengths are outweighed by analytic weaknesses which severely limit its value as an adequate explanatory model. That is not to say that social work, and other forms of welfare provision, may not have the effect of facilitating system integration and social integration. But such functions need not necessarily support an industrial logic type of analysis. The outcome of state social work for example may, in large or small part, be the more or less successful integration of individuals and, to use the functionalist code, societal subsystems into the overall social system. Indeed it may even be argued that such outcomes reflect the intentions behind state social work and other welfare provision. Even then, however, the crucial question that remains unanswered relates to whether such integrationist intentions and outcome are responses to the logic of industrialism or responses, to other dominant social forces in 'advanced' industrial societies.

Welfare, Social Work and the Radical Right

In recent years the views of the radical right on welfare, as on other areas of state intervention, have become part of the currency of the welfare, as well as the political, debate. A perspective, traditionally regarded with hostility by adherents to a wide range of views on the political spectrum, has been presented as the new political orthodoxy. The state provision of welfare and of much else has been characterized by the radical right as the source of many of Britain's social, economic and moral problems. The natural state of humankind is seen, from this perspective, as one in which individuals are free from regulation by the state (Hayek, 1980) and free to express natural individualism (Hayek, 1949).

State welfare, however, has functioned to limit individual freedom severely and also to place an economic burden on the British economy which has ultimately led to a fiscal crisis.

Once more, this approach appears to have much descriptive validity. With an elegance of rhetoric it offers an explanation of the failure of the British economy and the restructuring of welfare since the late 1960s. Social expenditure on welfare and other state activities in the postwar period had eaten up a growing proportion of gross national product. The non-productive sectors of the economy were, therefore, sapping the lifeblood of the productive sectors. The welfare state, in other words, had undermined the British economy. Such an analysis presents at least a *prima facie* case to be answered (see Bacon and Eltis, 1976, for an extended discussion of this issue).

Radical right views also emphasize the extent to which the provision of state welfare limits individual freedom to choose and also generates social cleavages. Authors from quite different political perspectives have argued that such views of state welfare are shared by the public at large (Klein, 1974; Harris and Seldon, 1979).

Only in a free market economy, argue the proponents of this approach, will freedom be assured and social and economic ills remedied.

Readers may, however, judge that the progress of this juggernaut theory of state and welfare has been somewhat impeded by the road blocks of empirical research and the speed restrictions imposed by a basic understanding of social structure.

Implicit in Friedman's analysis of welfare as obliterating human freedom is the proposition that in the free market society, which the radical right poses in contradistinction to the welfare state society, freedom would be a natural concomitant of social and economic organization. In doing so Friedman follows neo-classical economic theory which equates individual liberty with freedom. This must surely be a dubious equation because it ignores the effect that economic systems have on the distribution of power. The indisputable evidence to be drawn from the study of contemporary societies is that control of resources, especially of resources that are privately owned, gives resource holders disproportionate power. Radical right economists and social theorists, like the neo-classical economists before them, ignore in their analysis that the freedom of the individual is contingent on the place that the individual occupies in the social structure.

As we have seen, another important plank in the radical right analysis and critique is that welfare is socially disruptive. It translates wants and needs into rights. It is unable to satisfy demand for those rights and thus creates social cleavages between would-be recipients of services. It would certainly appear that the general public regards some state services and benefits as directed inappropriately. Certainly, public attitudes to, say, the practice of income maintenance agencies supports the contentions of the radical right in this instance (Klein, 1974; Taylor-Gooby, 1985). It is, nonetheless, the case that surveys of public opinion demonstrate these contentions to be only partly sustainable. Recent evidence suggests that in respect of large areas of state provision (for example, in health and education) public attitudes support further taxation and thence social expenditure to secure wider rights of access to welfare services (Taylor-Gooby, 1985).

A further set of arguments marshalled by the radical right is concerned with the effect of welfare spending on the so-called productive sectors of the economy. Large scale state welfare provision, it is argued, reduces the incentive of entrepreneurial individuals to innovate. It is said to do so because, like all services provided as a result of public expenditure, it implies high levels of taxation and thus restricted levels of reward for the successful entrepreneur. Additionally, it is argued, welfare expenditure has no discernible positive impact on production. The former claim remains unsupported by any reliable evidence and there may, in fact, be evidence which strongly suggests that taxation does not reduce incentive to any great extent (Galbraith, 1963). The second argument is a little more difficult to despatch. Direct links between expenditure on welfare and wealth production are difficult to trace. However, a consideration of the stated aims of certain social policies as aids to wealth creation may serve to cast some doubt on this particular anti-collectivist view.

A *prima facie* case can be constructed which offers strong suggestive evidence that social policies and welfare expenditure have, in fact, been used to create amenable conditions for increased industrial production and thence increased profit. Certainly, certain income maintenance and education policies introduced before the current economic recession would, at the very least, suggest that the industrial sector of the economy, as well as interventionist governments, perceived links between social expenditure and production and profit levels. One of the key pressure groups promoting the idea of a reorganization of state secondary education in the late 1950s and early 1960s was industrialists. A consistent complaint from the captains of British industry in the postwar period was that the then existing segregated system of secondary education acted as a brake on increased industrial production. It did so because that system failed to produce a reservoir of technologically competent industrial workers. A more flexible system of secondary education, such as that envisaged in the plans for comprehensivization, was regarded by British industrialists as more likely to improve levels of production and profit in British industry (see Bellaby, 1977; Reynolds and Sullivan, 1986).

Similarly, income maintenance provisions including the original Beveridge proposals and the introduction, in 1966, of an earnings related unemployment benefit provide highly suggestive evidence of a perceived link between social intervention and expenditure on the one hand and production and profit on the other. The immediate postwar provisions, set in the context of technical, if not actual, full employment may be seen as having served two functions. In the first place they provided an economic safety net to catch the frictionally unemployed and other minority groups. Secondarily they provided a level of income for those whose earnings had been interrupted which maintained basic levels of consumption. Domestic levels of consumption, in an economy which had been severely damaged by the burdens of war, were not insignificantly associated with levels of production and profit.

The introduction of an earnings related unemployment benefit took place interestingly enough at a historical juncture when the British economy was in the throes of an attempted move from labour intensive to capital intensive production. Government and state presented this social policy innovation as one which would help maintain the living standards of frictionally unemployed people. Evidence exists, however, which suggests that government, state and industry saw the new benefit as both placating those made unemployed by the restructuring of British industry and as maintaining domestic levels of consumption for more profitably produced products.

The above examples do not, of course, demonstrate beyond contradiction that certain social policies did aid the production and profit process. They do, however, suggest that state, government and industry in postwar Britain intended that they should. There are therefore strong grounds to regard the radical right analysis, in this area at least, as strikingly unpersuasive.

One final weakness of this approach relates to its implicit analysis of the relationship between state and government. Like the reformist and industrial state perspectives, this perspective theorizes the state as occupying a subservient or handmaiden position to government. Government, acting on a mandate from the population, makes policy, the organs of state execute that policy. Such a perspective would, therefore, suggest that governments pledged, like the Thatcher governments, to removing the state from substantial areas of interventionist activity in welfare might effect that intention more or less successfully. As we have seen in earlier chapters, the project of rolling back the state from substantial areas of welfare remains, despite the considerable restructuring of state activities, significantly incomplete (see also Taylor-Gooby, 1985). Whether this failure to determine state activity arises as a result of an underestimation, in theory and action, of the degree of state power which has passed out of the hands of government in contemporary British society (Jessop, 1980; Cawson 1982), or results from other factors, it does indicate a marked weakness in the radical right perspective on state and welfare.

Social workers may, as a consequence of the manifest weakness of this approach, regard it as of little use in charting either the past history or the future prospects of state social work. Its residual strengths may, however, be paradoxically useful for social work as theory and practice. The radical right perspective certainly fails to provide a comprehensive and entirely plausible analysis of state interventionist activities. At the level of description, however, it highlights a number of salient features about recipients' experience of welfare. At this level, it appears to share with much of the literature from the Marxist left a facility to uncover the paradoxes of welfare in a social democratic state. Though welfare provision, including the provision of state social work, has been presented in the literature and rhetoric of social democracy as state effort to improve the access of the whole population to the rights of living and civilized society, it has, at the same time increased state control over the lives of individuals (Boyson, 1971) and families (Mount, 1982). Additionally there appears to be reasonably supported evidence of client alienation from welfare services which is testimony to the descriptive if not the analytic strength of this approach (Taylor-Gooby, 1985). This perspective on state, welfare and social work might, then, be regarded as fundamentally weak as an explanatory model. Its description of some of the effects of state welfare on recipients, however, exposes issues which any satisfactory model of state, welfare and social work must address.

Marxism, Welfare and Social Work

In earlier chapters readers have been familiarized or refamiliarized with Marxist views on state, welfare and social work. It has been suggested that such Marxist views tend to fall either within a Marxist functionalist strand of analysis or within a more dialectical form of analysis which highlights the relative autonomy of the state and the role of political struggle in the development and functions of, often contradictory, state activities.

Those writing from a Marxist functionalist perspective tend, on the whole, to anchor their analysis of state welfare and state social work in a number of core assumptions about the nature of society and state which present welfare as no more than one of a number of state apparatuses utilized by a ruling class to reproduce the social, economic and political relationships of capitalist society.

As an explanatory model, Marxist functionalism has a number of considerable strengths. One of its major strengths is, quite simply, that its understandings of state and society are rooted in an analysis of history as well as of contemporary society. Unlike most other functionalist accounts, it seeks to locate social phenomena by establishing their place in historical patterns of societal development. The dynamic of history replaces the largely static snapshots of functionalist accounts of contemporary society in an attempt to provide holistic explanations. In consequence it is, for example, able to explain Marshall's development of citizen rights in capitalist society (Marshall, 1963) in a wider context. The struggle for civil, political and social rights is to be understood as a struggle between social classes in which subordinate social classes have sought to promote and increase their interests and influence in capitalist society. The responses of state and society to such struggles are to be understood as responses which ultimately protect the interests of a ruling class; for the package of citizen rights which emerged over three centuries of British history constituted not only the ransom paid by a ruling class in return for social stability but also, paradoxically, reinforced the interests of those in control. The granting of citizen rights is seen, from this perspective, as contributing to the social integration of society by attributing to all citizens equality of membership of the societal community whilst, at the same time, legitimating wider and more significant inequalities in economic power, resources and influence.

The Marxist functionalist model also appears to provide a persuasive analysis of the aims and functions of social policy. The impact of many social policies, it is claimed in many studies, has been, at best, to redistribute resources and life chances horizontally (within social classes) and, at worst, to protect and increase the allocation of resources and life chances to already privileged sections of the population (Halsey, Heath and Ridge, 1980; Townsend and Davidson, 1982; George and Wilding, 1984). From a Marxist functionalist standpoint this is easily explained. If the state provision of welfare is seen, in essence, as a strategy employed to protect and reinforce capitalism at a particular stage of its development, then it is unsurprising that the outcomes of social policy are largely consistent with intentions.

Marxist functionalism also rounds out the understandings of state intervention in economy and welfare provided by the functionalist industrial state approach. The original 'decisions' of societies to develop an industrial economy referred to by Galbraith (Galbraith, 1972) are exposed not as decisions but as determined by the development of capitalism as a social and economic system. The logic of industrialism (Kerr *et al.*, 1962) which is seen in the former approach to have determined the nature and scope of state intervention in society is unmasked. State interventionist policies have served the interests not of industrialism but of capitalism. State welfare interventions, as well as interventions in economic policy, have been determined by the capitalist state's promotion of the ruling class interests of capital accumulation and social stability.

This approach also provides a much more plausible account of the restructuring of state activities in recent years than does any of the previously considered perspectives. Capitalism has entered a new stage, in part precipitated by the increasingly difficult task of maintaining the dual processes of accumulation and legitimation through state interventionist strategies (O'Connor, 1973). The development of capitalism in the late twentieth century has also included the diminishing need for labour intensive manufacturing industries. As a consequence welfare interventionism has been removed, reduced or reoriented. Emphasis on, for example, industrial training rather than on liberal education is likely to provide the technologically proficient personnel of a much shrunken labour market. Removal of the 1966 Earnings Related Unemployment Benefit and the proposals included in the White Paper on Social Security (HMSO, 1986) are likely to encourage the unemployed into low paid service sector jobs. Increased social expenditure on coercive state agencies is to be seen as late capitalism's response to the potential of social unrest.

Notwithstanding these apparently considerable strengths, Marxist functionalism constructs a model for understanding state, society and welfare which also contains fundamental analytic weaknesses. Its main weaknesses are threefold. The first weakness is rooted in the all-pervading determinism of the model. Although the model explicitly presents a theory of history and social change which understands the dynamic for social change to be social class struggle, the prospect of successful working class struggle is largely absent in the fine detail of the model. Historical and contemporary struggles between the two major social classes and between other social groups are seen implicitly, if not explicitly, as capable of resolution only by the victory of a dominant social class or group aided by the state. As we have observed earlier, the struggle for citizen rights is seen as having elicited a response from the capitalist state aimed at, and largely successful in, incorporating all sections of the British population into the logic and values of capitalism (Saville, 1957; Mandel, 1968; Baran and Sweezy, 1968). Struggles for state welfare provision have resulted in similar outcomes. The capitalist state has utilized the struggles for state provided health, education, income maintenance and other services to develop a welfare system which has functioned to satisfy the needs of capitalism rather than the needs of ordinary people. Social welfare interventions, whether in education, health or income maintenance, are seen as responses to changing labour force needs or changing market needs of capitalist enterprise. State policies in relation to education, social work and income maintenance provision are seen as having been determined, in large part, by the need to reinforce and recreate the norms and values of capitalist society. The provision of base-line income maintenance services and services in cash and kind are seen as part of a strategy of system maintenance and as a buffer against social unrest (see Chapter 3).

Whilst this sort of approach has a kind of all-inclusive explanatory neatness about it, it poses problems on theoretical and empirical levels. In the first place it is, paradoxically, profoundly unMarxist. It purports to be rooted in a set of social theories which have abstracted from the observation of social realities the lesson that progressive social change will occur as a result of the social and political struggles of a strong working class movement. Nonetheless, in its detailed analysis of historical and contemporary struggles for welfare, it presents as rigid a puppet theatre model of state, society and welfare as the functionalist inspired industrial state approach considered earlier. The capitalist puppeteer (the state), acting on instructions from its employer (the ruling class), determines the outcome of each societal drama as surely as the beachside entertainer controls the outcome of each and every conflict between Punch and Judy. With the help of repressive or ideological state apparatuses (Althusser, 1971) – capitalist society's equivalent of the sometimes stern, sometimes caring policeman – the ruling class controls, or uses to its own advantage, the actions of the working class movement (Punch and Judy) even when those actions (political struggle) appear, as in each and every seaside performance, to be aimed at overthrowing the rule of law and the conventions of dominant society.

At an empirical level, the approach is equally unsatisfactory. The history of state welfare provision is a history marked by the selective opposition of large sections of industrial capitalism to state expenditure on welfare and by cacophonous complaints that welfare policies have failed, even if that were the intention, to service the needs of capitalism. The empirical realities of postwar Britain, then, provide weak rather than strong foundations on which to build the Marxist functionalist edifice.

Other weaknesses are also evident in this perspective. On a theoretical level, it fails to give any satisfactory explanation of the claim that the state in capitalist society always acts to serve the interests of a capitalist class. On an empirical level, it appears to ignore any evidence which suggests that the state, even on rare occasions, has intervened in civil society in ways which may not have reinforced or protected the interests of a capitalist class exclusively. An extensive literature now exists which suggests that state interventions in economy and welfare have at times appeared to reflect the interests of a constituency wider than, though often including, a ruling or capitalist class (see Chapter 3; and, for example, Offe and Ronge, 1975; Corrigan and Leonard, 1978; Ginsburg, 1979; Gough, 1979; Offe, 1982). The questions raised in such work are seldom addressed in the Marxist functionalist model.

Finally, the fundamental basis of this perspective appears to be little more than a tautology. The state in capitalist society is presented as a political directorate co-ordinating the interests of capitalism. Its main function is seen as the perpetuation of a capitalist system of social, economic and political organization. The perpetuation of a capitalist system is seen as sufficient evidence of both the function of the state in capitalist societies and of its successful execution of that function. Consequently, all state activity is seen as necessarily determined, in intention and in outcome, by the state's *raison d'être* – the perpetuation of the capitalist system. Explanations of the durability of capitalism as a social and economic system which do not emphasize the pre-eminent role played by a ruling class, through the mechanisms of the state, in maintaining that system are rarely considered and more rarely evaluated.

Those involved in the practice of social work may experience a sense of relief that the Marxist functionalist edifice is constructed on less secure foundations than is first apparent. Such relief that the functions of social work, as soft policing or ideological indoctrination into the norms and values of capitalism, are open to question might, however, be short lived. For it remains imperative that we seek to understand the contradictions apparent in state welfare activities and to perceive the weaknesses of understandings which see welfare as the activity of a benign state to meet identified need.

An increasingly strong body of evidence exists which indicates that an adequate understanding of the relationship between society, state and welfare must, whilst avoiding the rigid determinism of Marxist functionalism, account for an apparent tendency for the state to act primarily in the interests of dominant or ruling sections of the population. Such an understanding would also need to suggest how, given such a relationship, some of the interests of a wide societal constituency may also be met, albeit secondarily and contingently, by the state.

As we have seen, a number of writers (Miliband, 1969; 1978; 1982; Poulantzas, 1972; 1975; Offe and Ronge, 1975; Ginsburg, 1979; Gough, 1797; Offe, 1984) all present analyses which suggest two important features of the modern capitalist state. First, it is suggested that the state in capitalist societies is predisposed to act in the long term interests of capitalism. But secondly, it is argued, with varying emphasis, that the state does possess a degree of relative autonomy from ruling interests and is particularly susceptible to change at times of heightened inter-class or intra-class struggle.

In order to come to some tentative conclusions about the strength of this perspective as an explanatory model we need to give some consideration to the evidence.

It has been argued that the conditions under which postwar state welfare has been developed suggests support for the idea of a constrained but relatively autonomous state intervening in ways which demonstrate it to be acting in a tension between antagonistic and contradictory influences (Offe, 1984). As a consequence, it is argued, the policies that emerge from the state are contradictory in their aims and functions.

The thirty-year period following the Second World War might serve to test this hypothesis. During this period the British economy underwent an unprecedented expansion which led to both the depletion of labour reserves and to an increasingly strong labour movement. This period also saw an expansion in the range and functions of state intervention. There appears to be a *prima facie* case, at least, for an explanatory model which suggests:

(1) that, during this period, interventionist policies were placed on the political agenda in response to labour movement pressure thus demonstrating a degree of relative autonomy for the state;
     and

(2) that the nature of the policies developed were, despite their provenance, deeply contradictory.

As we have seen earlier (Chapter 3), this might be seen to be reflected in policies on education (see p. 85), housing (see p. 86) and income maintenance (see p. 89). Similarly, state social work, emerging out of the welfare state package, appears to have served contradictory functions during this period. An emphasis on rehabilitation rather than punishment quite clearly emerged in postwar social work (Packman, 1975; Jones, 1983). At the same time, however, an emphasis on ideas of family rather than structural pathology as the source of social ills (Jenkins, 1972; Joseph, 1972) placed social work practice equally clearly within the conformative apparatus of the state (Pearson, 1973; Corrigan and Leonard, 1978; Jones, 1983).

The changing focus of social work during the subsequent retrenchment of the economy in the 1970s and 1980s would also, on the face of it, point towards a model of understanding dependent on notions of relative autonomy and contradiction.

The establishment of unified social service departments in the early 1970s might well be seen as demonstrating both the relative autonomy of the state to act in the interests of a wide societal constituency and also the constraints within which that autonomy operated. In part, the Seebohm Committee's proposals reflected an acceptance of a structural pathology explanation of social problem causation. The 'rediscovery of poverty' school of thought appears to have convinced the committee that many of the problems social work confronted were socially rather than individually induced. The state, itself, acted to implement the universal departments which the committee saw as providing universalistic services but did so in a way (and with such resources) which limited the focus of intervention to the level of the family and served to entrench the notion of family pathology as the cause of social ills.

The development of community work may also be seen as highlighting similar contradictions. State sanctioned and financed community work may legitimately be seen as emerging as a strategy to integrate socially potentially alienated sections of British society. The decline of industry, especially in inner-city areas during the late 1960s, formed part of the restructuring of capitalism. It also appears to have precipitated a sense of alienation among those who lived in such areas who experienced, following the demise of indigenous industry, high levels of poverty, unemployment, housing problems and environmental blight. In such situations, the local and central state was perceived to have lost its legitimacy for at least certain sections of the population. The capitalist state, and indeed ruling interests, were therefore faced with a paradoxical problem. Capital accumulation must, perforce, be fostered but there was also a clear and urgent need to integrate socially a potentially malcontent inner-city working class. Community work was seen as the solution to this paradox (Bolger *et al.*, 1981; Loney, 1983). Community work was to function as a shock absorber to incorporate poor working class areas into mainstream society and to manage or mediate conflict between damaged communities and the local state (Gough, 1979). Community work projects, once established, were to operate within an ideology of community pathology and were to work to modify this pathology through facilitating community self-help. That this was the intention may well be demonstrated by the fate of radical Community Development Projects which developed a structural understanding of social problems (Loney, 1983). Nonetheless, this example of welfare intervention can be seen as illustrating both the relative autonomy of the state and also the contradictory nature of welfare intervention.

That such projects and communities were resourced in the first place may well reflect the state's capacity to respond to perceived threat. That state financed community work was expected to develop a community pathology focussed practice, aimed at social integration, may well demonstrate the limits of that autonomy. Nonetheless, it may be argued that British community work in the 1970s and 1980s exposes the full limits of autonomy.

Contemporary community work represents much more than an ideological charade. In order for community work to function successfully in the interests of capitalism it has perforce to develop real and direct relationships with working class people and communities. In doing so it exposes a crucial contradiction which exists at the core of welfare provision: even interventions intended to control and integrate carry some potential for liberation. To develop direct relationships with the community in which they work community workers introduce the possibility of participation and dialogue on community and wider issues. Policies and actions related to the long term concerns of ruling interests have, nonetheless, on a number of issues from housing to employment contained the promise – and sometimes the reality – of power through knowledge and participation (see Craig, Derricourt and Loney, 1982; Loney, 1983).

Welfare intervention may, then, expose a tension between the long term interests of capitalism on the one hand and the interests of a wider constituency on the other. Further room for manoeuvre may exist in a degree of autonomy for practitioners from the state context in which they work. We move on, in the next chapter, to explore whether a sociological imagination in social work practice might expand the boundaries of that autonomy.

6 Sociological Imagination and the Practice of Social Work

In the last chapter we concluded that state welfare and the practice of social work, though constrained, are not completely determined by the interests, values and ideologies of a dominant social class. State social work, it was suggested, operates within a tension between, on the one hand, the requirements of capitalism and, on the other, the capacity of the state to act relatively autonomously from those interests. In other words, a proposition emerged that there is a potentially incomplete fit between the interests of a dominant class and the practice of state sanctioned social work and other welfare activities. Such an analysis has led some to pose the strategy of working 'in and against the state' (London Edinburgh Weekend Return Group, 1980), or to see a conflict in welfare policy and activity between the values of social democracy and the values of free market capitalism (Bolger *et al.*, 1981; Jones, 1983).

This chapter represents an attempt to explore ways in which such an incomplete fit can be exploited by social workers in order to provide positive help to the clients of social work. It will be argued that sociological theory and sociological imagination form invaluable weapons in the struggle for this critical and reflective social work practice.

The chapter will focus on three areas of social work practice: work relating to poverty; work with children and families; and social work with those labelled as mentally ill. In each case it will be suggested that a sociologically informed practice presents workers with the possibility of transcending a view of social work as a series of cases (Mills, 1943) and of practising in ways consistent with the needs of clients and the contexts in which they live their lives.

Poverty and Welfare

As we have seen in previous chapters, modern social work has developed, in part, out of fears about the threat to social stability posed by an impoverished underclass. During the twentieth century explanations of poverty appear, as we have already noted, to have shifted from an emphasis on moral degeneracy as a causative factor to a tendency to understand the perpetuation of poverty in terms of the psychological or social inadequacy of the poor (Lewis, 1961; Joseph, 1972). In consequence, ways of dealing with the poor have changed – often gradually and sometimes imperceptibly – from punitive strategies to strategies of rehabilitation or resocialization. Poverty in welfare state Britain has spawned a considerable social welfare related literature which, despite the rediscovery of poverty in the 1960s, often promotes the idea of poverty as a form of individual, family, or community inadequacy. Poverty has been said to persist as a result of a cycle of deprivation which has the effect of transmitting the behaviour of deprivation – inadequate parenting, lack of achievement motivation, unemployability, present time orientation and the like – from one generation to another (Joseph, 1972). Alternatively, the persistence of poverty has been understood as stemming from the incapacity of whole communities of people to adapt to changing industrial processes and developments. The poor become and stay poor because they lack the qualities necessary to climb out of poverty (see Loney, 1983, for an eloquent critique of this approach).

Social work activity has therefore tended to focus on interventions intended to change the attitudes, functioning and behaviour of the poor as families or as communities (a process documented in various ways by Jordan, 1974; 1981; Loney, 1983; Mack and Lansley, 1985). Despite the recognition of structural causes of poverty by the Seebohm Committee on social services and despite a substantial research literature reinforcing structural explanations of poverty (Townsend and Abel-Smith, 1965; Coates and Silburn, 1970; 1983; Rutter and Madge, 1977; Holman, 1978; Townsend, 1979; Jordan, 1981), social work practice and the attitudes which inform it have remained strangely impervious to explanations which question the importance of individual family or community pathology in explaining poverty. Social service department work with the poor is often reduced to concepts and actions rooted in a victim blaming ideology (Ryan, 1971) which emphasizes the need to rescue and, if possible, rehabilitate the poor into the expectations of mainstream society. One example will suffice to demonstrate this point. Despite relatively recent evidence (NSPCC, 1984) of a *prima-facie* association between levels of unemployment and levels of child abuse, statutory procedures and social work practice in this area seem to be informed by a crude model of individual or family pathology. Specifically, both the assumption by government and social work agencies that certain types of family are more likely to abuse, and the implicit connection made between predictive factors in child abuse and explicit factors said to be associated with a cycle of deprivation, constitute a model for intervention predicated on blaming the victim. Certain families in our society are seen as especially vulnerable to the experience of poverty. They are so because they are the victims of a process of intergenerational transmission of deficient behaviour. That deficient behaviour, in turn, makes them more likely to be the perpetrators or victims of child abuse as they are less likely to possess the qualities needed for good parenting. Such a model, of course, avoids the need to consider any apparent association between social structure and this particular sort of seemingly private trouble (see Parton and Thomas, in Jordan and Parton, 1983). Social work policies and practice may, then, reflect dominant ideas about poverty. They may also serve to reinforce them.

It is in such a context that the use of a sociological imagination might contribute to a social work practice intended to help clients rather than to reinforce dominant ideas. A sociological perspective might aid the practitioner at three levels:

(1) It might help the practitioner to move behind taken-for-granted assumptions and in so doing to articulate the relationship between social structure on the one hand and the experience and behaviour of poverty on the other.

(2) It may help to explain the persistence of a social welfare ideology resistant to those understandings.

(3) It may point the way to appropriately critical and reflective practice with those who experience poverty.

Social Structure and the Experience of Poverty

The persistence of poverty in capitalist society, even at times of relative affluence, has appeared paradoxical to some social workers and some politicians. Every social worker could attest to the apparent intergenerational transmission of poverty and associated problems among particular sections of the population. The multi-problem family experiencing and manifesting financial, personal and social problems from one generation to another appears to give credence to an understanding of poverty rooted in the idea of individual or family inadequacies. The idea that problem families cause their problems rather than merely experiencing them has become the commonsense folklore of social work agencies and social workers. Social work attitudes may have shifted from a perspective which held that 'indigence was simply the punishment meted out to the improvident by their own lack of industry and efficiency . . . poverty was the obvious consequence of sloth and sinfulness' (Bremner, in Weinberger, 1974), but often seem to have become stuck at a point which suggests family pathology as responsible for poverty, loose morals, drunkenness, delinquency, criminality and child neglect (Philp, 1963). The value of a sociological perspective at this level is to aid the critical practitioner in a process of debunking commonsense understandings where they need to be debunked and also in a process of theory construction. The practitioner working with people in poverty needs, as a first step towards reflective practice, to build up a theoretical understanding of poverty which accounts for the micro-features of poverty (apparently inadequate child rearing, perceptions of alienation and the like) as well as accounting for the persistence of poverty at a macro-level. This process of constructing plausible accounts, then, might take place in three stages.

The first of these stages is one of critical evaluation of sociological and other social science research on the causes of poverty. The main features of this stage would include, in the first place, looking behind the research findings which sustain particular theories of poverty to unearth the processes which yield those findings. Doubts about the potency of family pathology explanations may be induced if one considers the failure of much of the early cycle of deprivation research to investigate family poverty in a rigorous fashion (a prime example of this early work can be found in Lidbetter, 1933). Wooton, writing as far back as 1959, itemized the weaknesses of such research. According to her it utilized vague and subjective concepts of poverty, it failed to compare the lives of the poor with those of the non-poor, it failed to measure the recurrence of supposed intergenerational deprivation over time (Wooton, 1959). Such research might be seen as demonstrating little more than a catalogue of methodological failures.

Similarly, more recent research which has at times appeared to point towards a cultural deprivation explanation of poverty is based on dubious methodological foundations. Lewis (1961) had suggested that the poorest sections of society formed a subculture of poverty which was distinctive and self-perpetuating. This hypothesis suggested that 'remarkable similarities in family structure, interpersonal relations . . . value systems, spending patterns . . . in lower class settlements in London, Glasgow, Paris, Harlem and Mexico City' (Lewis, 1961, p. xxvi) reflected a subculture of society which inculcated each generation into the distinct values of a culture of poverty. Yet, the weight of sociological inquiry seems to suggest that almost all the criteria adopted here in distinguishing a subculture of poverty from mainstream culture are inexact, contradictory, or value loaded (see Valentine, 1968; Townsend, 1974).

However plausible these approaches might have appeared to

the practitioner at first sight, a critical evaluation of the research which sustains them may, at least, lead to an element of doubt about their status as satisfactory explanatory models. The practitioner may be drawn, therefore, to utilize the sociological imagination to construct understandings of poverty perpetuation which have apparently greater validity. In so doing s/he will have to consider the findings of more rigorously executed sociological work. If relatively large pockets of poverty have persisted in a society like Britain even at times of relative affluence, if the scope of poverty has expanded alarmingly in the recession years, then the practitioner will need to consider findings which suggest that poverty and inequality are inherent features of capitalist social organization with its emphasis on the values of individual freedom rather than on substantive equality (Holman, 1978; Townsend, 1979). S/he will need to consider very carefully the apparent functions of the social services (Holman, 1978), the education system (Halsey, Heath and Ridge, 1980) and the media (Holman, 1978) as mechanisms of perpetuating and legitimizing poverty and inequality.

Such evaluative sociological inquiry may then lead on to a further stage. That stage may attempt a reconceptualization of the behaviours and attitudes of poor people. It may well be that, at least on one level, the work of the culture of poverty theorists has validity. Poor people and poor communities do often appear to display quite separate and distinct behaviours from those of the non-poor. Child-rearing patterns do appear different – sometimes more rigid, sometimes more lax – than those of the non-poor. Spending patterns and achievement motivations sometimes do appear to the practitioner as markedly different among the poor and the non-poor. One of the crucial questions that the sociologically aware practitioner will be asking at this point in the process relates, however, to the plausibility of the culture of poverty theorists' analysis of these apparent differences. Their descriptive validity may not be in doubt but the sociological imagination will prod the social worker to ask a further series of questions about whether the behaviours of poverty in relation to child-rearing (see Wilson and Herbert, 1978), spending patterns (see Coates and

Silburn, 1970) or deferral of gratification mark the presence of separate value systems to that held by other sections of the population, or whether they may simply be rational adaptations of behaviour to inauspicious social circumstances (Holman, 1978).

The worker so far may have exploited a sociological imagination to question commonsense understandings of poverty and to perceive poverty's objective and subjective meanings. The result may be to lead him/her to a conceptualization of poor people as victims of a social system predicated on inequality. These people may be seen as adopting the characteristics of internal aliens in a society which excludes them from access to the modicum of economic security enjoyed by others.

Sociology and Social Welfare Systems

Sociological curiosity might also lead the practitioner to explore reasons for the apparent resistance of social welfare institutions to non-pathological understandings of poverty causation and perpetuation. That curiosity might lead to a consideration of the part played by clinical psychiatric models of social problems in the development of social work's identity and increasing professionalization (see Chapter 7; and Heraud, 1970). It may also lead to a consideration of the relationship between social classes, the state and welfare. The worker will wish to explore the ideological and material significance of welfare's failure to redistribute resources. The critical worker will wish to analyse whether anti-poverty policies based on cycle of deprivation theories actually signify a strong tendency for the state to act in ways which both promote the interests of the economically powerful and relocate the responsibility for poverty from the level of structure to the level of the individual, family, or community. In doing so, those within social work who wish to reflect on their theory and practice will also wish to analyse whether such state actions, and the values they reflect, represent relatively progressive or relatively retrograde developments in relation to previous attitudes and actions of poverty.

The worker may therefore be forced to concede after reflection that social work agencies and social workers themselves operate within a material reality and a set of ideologies which significantly constrain their capacity to alleviate the problems of poverty, let alone liberate the poor.

The critical social worker may, however, wish to use a developed sociological awareness to take his or her explorations still further. The question that may be asked is this: 'notwithstanding the overall interests of the economically powerful, does a tension exist between the intentions of policies – arguably designed to protect those interests – on the one hand, and the rehabilitative emphasis of postwar social work?' The sociological imagination may illuminate a chink of relative autonomy even within the inauspicious context of 1980s Britain. It may lead the practitioner to posit a lack of complete fit between state action and state policies and the ideology and actions of a state sanctioned social work system. The tools of sociological inquiry may help to construct a plausible account which stresses the contradictory nature of state social work's value system: on the one hand it operates as a state agency with the functions of resocializing deviant or mal-integrated subgroups into the values of capitalist society and controlling those who cannot be socialized into conformity; at the same time it is characterized by a competing system of values, deeply rooted in the political philosophy of social democracy, which emphasizes self-determination (in the case of social case work), or participation and dialogue (in the case of state sanctioned community work). It may thus possess the capacity to work against, or at least to modify, the forces of conformity. The social worker may, as a result, become acutely aware of the welfare dialectic, of the potentially contradictory nature of social work policy and practice.

Sociology and Social Work Practice

In this context, the sociological imagination offers one further service to social work: it helps to delineate those methods of intervention which may act to increase levels of self-determination, participation and dialogue. It may, in other words, facilitate the social worker and the client (or group) to influence the welfare dialectic. The process of sociological inquiry so far will have allowed the worker to explore the root causes and the experience of poverty. Sociological research will have highlighted those groups within the population most vulnerable to structurally induced poverty: the elderly, the unskilled, lone parents and their families, ethnic minorities, etc. The worker will have become familiarized with the effects of poverty – physical exhaustion, ill health, social isolation, low self-esteem, a sense of defeat – from practice and from the poverty literature (Coates and Silburn 1970; 1983; Wilson and Herbert, 1978; Townsend, 1979; Mack and Lansley, 1985). He or she may, therefore, wish to avoid interventionist strategies that tend to pathologize what appear to be rational, if forced, adaptations to difficult social and individual situations. Areas of work may tend, therefore, to include those that facilitate a process of normalization of the experiences of the poor and a set of strategies to mitigate the worst effects of poverty. The worker may, consequently, focus on some or all of the following helping strategies:

Individual work: He or she may work with individuals in poverty to improve self-esteem and to debunk ideas of individual and/or family pathology as the determinants of poverty.

Work with groups: The worker may wish to facilitate the coming together of clients with similar experiences of poverty in order both to further normalize those experiences for clients and to establish dialogue between poor people in a particular area.

Consultancy: The worker may wish to make available

	knowledge and information about statutory agencies' resource allocation policies (or about key decision-making structures for resource allocation) in order to improve the likelihood of positive outcome in any campaign or participatory process between local groups of the poor and resource holders.
Social skills work:	It may be found useful to work with poor people as individuals or groups to improve social skills. This process may be seen as particularly useful in improving skills of negotiation, confrontation, etc.
Advocacy:	There may be times when it is regarded as appropriate for the social worker to act as advocate for the poor person or family. This might be a particularly useful form of intervention in negotiations with income maintenance agencies.

Such strategies, prompted by the insights of sociological theory and practice, may be seen as pushing the worker to the boundaries between professional and political work. Such an ambiguous role might be uncomfortable for many practitioners, but often seems inescapable for reflective and conscious workers in a social welfare system itself rooted in contradictions.

Client centred, sociologically informed practice in the areas of child and family work and work with the 'mentally ill' is likely to expose similar conflicts and contradictions for the social worker to negotiate.

Social Work and the Family

The emphasis on appropriate mother-centred child-rearing practices in social work has been argued to be more to do with the regulation of women's lives than with successful negotiation of childhood (Wilson, 1977, ch. 4; Brook and Davis, 1985, ch. 3). Sociological inquiry almost inevitably takes the informed social worker behind the taken-for-granted assumptions about universal and normal child-rearing practices present in much of the earlier social work literature (Bowlby 1953; Robertson, 1962) and in much present social work practice. The sociological imagination propels the social worker to search the literature on child-rearing either to track down this much sought-after holy grail, or to become convinced of its non-existence. The research literature on other contemporary cultures (Bronfenbrenner, 1974, on the USSR; and Bettelheim, 1969, on child-rearing in the Kibbutz, for instance) will elicit at least a degree of scepticism about the universality or normality of mother-centred child-rearing in the nuclear family. Some of the British literature (and, especially, Rutter, 1975) will raise significant questions about the assumed harmful effects on children of multiple bond relationships early in life. Other literature (see, especially, Rapoport, Rapoport and Strelitz, 1977) will indicate to the social worker the potential value to children of non-mother-centred parenting paradigms. The sociologically informed practitioner may, then, find that the sociological imagination raises questions fundamental to the theory and practice of social work with families. The worker may ask whether theories of maternal care (Ehrenreich and English, 1979) on which much social work activity with families appears to be based, are more closely associated with the social reproduction of a well-socialized workforce and with the perpetuation of conventional systems of gender relations than with the concepts of childhood need. Are such concepts, the sociologically informed social worker may ask, merely examples of normative theory about the structure and functions of the family, rather than attempts to understand and promote the healthy psychological and emotional development of children?

Sociological inquiry and conventional social work theory may, then, prove uncongenial bedfellows. Improved understanding of both the diversity of family practices in child-rearing and the social outcomes of apparently commonsense theory may, however, have significant implications for practice. As much statutory work with children and families depends, crucially, on the worker's judgement of any given family situation, the sociological imagination, the ability to establish other reference points to those provided by conventional understandings, may lead to a more conscious and reflective practice in the area.

Social Work and Mental Health

Similarly, the insights of sociology potentially enrich (as well as no doubt complicate) work with those labelled as mentally ill. Recent legislation has underlined the pivotal role to be played by appropriately trained and approved social workers. Such workers are charged with the responsibility of investigating and understanding the social and familial, as well as the individual, factors associated with the client with mental health problems. Crucially, these workers have the statutory responsibility of weighing these factors and the medical opinion of psychiatric specialists in coming to decisions about the appropriateness of hospital care in cases of apparent mental ill health (see Olsen, 1984, for greater detail).

Approved mental health social workers have, however, been given this function in the context of both a strong adherence to a medical model of mental illness by medical practitioners and a growing scepticism by some others about the nature of mental illness.

Tools which might, therefore, be regarded as essential in promoting client welfare and protecting client rights in this context must include elements of the sociological approach and sociological theory. In crucial work of this sort practice must, at least, be influenced by sociological as well as other understandings of the field of mental health.

At a general level the worker will need to attempt to unravel the social context of mental ill health. He or she will need, at the very least, to seek explanations for the inverse relationship between social class position and diagnosed mental illness (Hollingshead and Redlich, 1958; Brown and Harris, 1978) and the disproportionate representation of women in official records of mental ill health (see Dalton, 1969; Gove and Tudor, 1973; Oakley, 1974; Leeson and Gray, 1978, for a range of different explanations).

At the level of individual behaviour, the worker will need to evaluate critically other possible understandings of mental health to those provided by organic illness theories. The sociological imagination may, therefore, lead him/her to a conscious and reflective assessment of theories suggesting that mental illness constitutes little more than one form of recorded rule infraction (Scheff, 1968). It may also lead to a careful consideration of the plausibility of labelling perspectives which understand further rule infractions as self-fulfilling prophesies (Scheff, 1968). Good practice and sociological rigour will no doubt lead the practitioner to consider the influence of family relationships and interaction on the state of mind of the identified client. In this regard, he or she may wish to scrutinize the claims of the anti-psychiatrists and especially the work of Ronald Laing (Laing, 1975; Laing and Esterson, 1974).

In this area, as in the others considered in this chapter, the use of sociology may well lead the practitioner to pose questions with an acute relevance to practice. A sociological perspective, it may therefore be argued, is of particular use to the social work practitioner. Despite what might be seen as the mutual advantages of this interpenetration of sociological understanding and social work practice, the interpenetration of theory and practice is largely absent in much current social work practice. The concluding chapter of this book considers the possible reasons for this and constructs a case for a happier marriage between sociology and social work.

7 Sociology and Social Welfare: Problems and Prospects

The intention behind writing this book was to explore ways in which sociology, as an academic discipline and a set of analytic tools, might aid the theory and practice of social welfare. In earlier chapters an attempt has been made to show how and in what ways sociology aids the development of understanding of the aims and functions of social welfare systems, the development of social policies and the theory and practice of social work. It has been argued that sociology represents an invaluable analytic weapon in the armoury not only of social policy analysts but also of social work practitioners. Yet, historically, the association between sociology and social work has been uncomfortable. That discomfort persists in our present circumstances. Resistance to or suspicion about sociology's claims to enrich the theory and practice of social work are not solely the province of a political ultra-right fearing that sociology means, in effect, training in subversion. Social work employers and social work practitioners have often responded to the discipline with hostility, or have, in a somewhat more muted way, echoed Cohen's response that 'it's alright for you to talk' (Cohen, in Bailey and Brake, 1975, pp. 76–95). Social work educators have also joined the fray. Munday, a senior social work academic commenting on the contribution of sociology to social work, regrets its effect on the students because the student is exposed to 'general attacks on traditional beliefs in society . . . a variety of academic material that is threatening, undermining and often downright depressing' (Munday, 1972). In this Munday echoes Bailey's contention that the effect, if not the intention, of sociological contributions to social work training have tended to underline 'social workers' insecurities about the theoretical basis of their practice' (Bailey, 1980, p. 71). Sociologists have also often steered clear of social work education or applied research, preferring to leave that field to social administrators.

This concluding chapter is devoted to trying to understand the problems which sociology and social work perceive in a closer association between the two practices. It concludes by balancing those problems against the advantages, for both sociology and social work, of a closer association.

Sociology and Social Work: Problems

Problems relating to a greater interpenetration of sociological analysis and social work practice appear to fall into two categories: problems arising from the nature and history of social work practice and problems arising from the nature of sociologists' practice (see also Heraud, 1970, for a discussion of these issues).

Problems arising from the nature and history of social work seem to stem from four sets of factors. They may be summarized as

(1) a rejection of the utility of sociology to social work practice;
(2) an elevation of experience over theory;
(3) a tendency to see psychology and psychiatry as all-inclusive frameworks for understanding humans and human problems;
(4) a tendency to discredit sociology as a result of its apparent association with a critique of traditional social work practice.

Sociology Is Not Useful

If social work is hostile to or suspicious of the benefits of a sociologically informed practice, then one of the factors associated with such reactions may well arise from a resistance to seeing the practice of social work as anything but humane and instinctual in its nature. We have seen in Chapter 6 that attempts to apply a sociological imagination to understanding social problem causation and resolution may lead the social worker into forms of practice which entail working at the margins of perceived legitimacy, often blurring traditional boundaries between welfare and politics. Such insights, often the result of unpacking taken-for-granted understandings of the individual and social world, can be deeply disturbing and uncomfortable for the state sanctioned social worker. Equally importantly, however, such insights can be defined as practically useless. The process of defining them so may have much to do with a tradition in Western social work to perceive the social worker as professional altruist, reflecting the beneficent intent of society and state by working to reintegrate deviant or disorganized individuals and groups into a more or less just and harmonious society (Halmos, 1965). This particular construction of social reality facilitates a definition of sociology not simply as intellectually challenging but, more importantly, as intellectually and practically unconvincing. Social work, in adopting a stance of 'theoryless practice' (Bailey, 1980) invalidates any potential contribution from sociology.

Sociology Is No Substitute for Experience

If sociological analysis is seen as an unconvincing guide to the practice of a humane and instinctive altruism, then social workers may feel that the best preparation for social work practice is one which ignores the use of sociological insights altogether. Sociological insights, at worst irrelevant at best superfluous, are rejected in favour of the experience gained through living. Heraud records the attitude to sociological training of a mature American social worker with a varied and sometimes painful experience of life. Social science courses were, for her, 'as interesting as a trip in an aeroplane would be to a person who had walked over the area and knew every road and path by heart' (Heraud, 1970, p. 273).

At best then, sociology may be seen as replacing the sensitive, fine grain knowledge of human interaction gained by the social worker as experienced human being with the vague, the general and the unfocussed.

The Psychiatric Deluge

Another reason for the failure of sociology to make inroads into social work theory and practice may, perhaps, be found in the history of social work development.

During the 1940s and 1950s when social work in Britain was struggling to gain a professional identity, it became, as we have seen (Chapter 4), strongly associated with the individual and family pathology approaches to human problems adopted by clinical psychiatry. Arguably, such an identification was perceived as a short-cut to high professional status for social work. Without doubt, the effect of such an identification was to see society or culture, to which sociology insisted on addressing itself, as largely unimportant determinants of human problems. Even a short period of time spent in most social work offices, or indeed in some social work training courses, would serve to demonstrate that many social workers continue to cling tightly to the security of familiar psychiatric tenets, and how resistant social work as a profession may be to the enrichment that sociology may offer.

In effect, an over-identification with clinical psychiatry may have led many social workers to perceive as the totality of sociology what is, in fact, but an element of it. Many social workers may have seen sociology as, at best, providing more or less plausible accounts of macro-social processes. Micro-social processes, which are seen as being at the heart of social work, seem to them to be dealt with only by psychology and psychiatry. Sociology is mistakenly seen as concerned only with man in society rather than being concerned also with society in man.

Sociology and the Critique of Social Work

It is also undoubtedly the case that social work's perception of sociology stems from the latter's association with a critique of social work as a social practice intended to effect social control and social cohesion in an unequal society (Saville, 1957; O'Connor, 1973).

Sociology at its best is, indeed, a subversive discipline in that it constantly seeks the meanings which lie beneath taken-for-granted assumptions about behaviour, action and social structure. This debunking quality must lead to an ongoing critique of social work practice as of any practice. As a result sociology might be conceived of as 'bringing the Trojan Horse of criticism into social work practice' (Heraud, 1970). Sociology may raise questions about the implicit functions of individual therapy when practised in the context of apparently structurally induced problems. It may well demand a scrutiny of extra-individual as well as intra-individual determinants of human problems. It may guide the social worker to investigate the latent as well as the overt functions of welfare policy and institutions. Where traditional social work may be concerned with how problems are caused by individual or family malfunctioning, sociology may be concerned to raise questions about the social, political and economic context in which problems occur. Sociology, then, may be perceived by vested interests in social work as a threat to social work as traditionally practised rather than as an aid to critical practice.

This threat has been perceived by Mills, in a by now classic paper, as a threat to the traditional tendency of social workers and other professionals to individualize and pathologize problems which are often rooted in the structure of society. Whereas sociology encourages its students to analyse social problems by looking behind taken-for-granted commonsense assumptions,

> pathologists tend to slip past structures to focus on isolated situations. . . . Their activities and norms are set within the existent norms of society; in their professional work they tend to have an occupational incapacity to rise above a series of 'cases'. (Mills, 1943)

So, it may well be the case that the relative lack of interpenetration between sociology and social work is the result of a number of factors associated with the nature and history of social work itself. It is almost certainly true that it is also the result of a basic problem arising from sociologists' own role definition.

It does appear that, to a considerable extent, sociology has remained aloof from critical study of the empirical reality of social work practice. It may be that such toil in the grubby reality of the welfare world is seen as leaving the academic sociologist not only grimy but also drawn away from the central concerns of theory generation. It may be that the earlier growth of social administration as a discipline associated with social work has acted as a brake on involvement. Whatever the reasons, sociology has danced coyly at the margins of social work despite the advantages that may accrue to both as a result of closer association. It is to these advantages that we now turn.

In essence what is argued in the rest of this chapter is that the practice of social work needs the sociological imagination and that sociology as a discipline needs social work.

As we have seen in the previous chapter, the process of interpretation in social work can gain from the sociological stance. Specifically, sociology as a discipline gives the sociologist, and could aid in social workers the development of, the following skills:

(1) the ability to take on the role of the outsider – to take a greater distance from the traumatic situations social workers often face than is often possible when we take the role of friend or contemporary;

(2) the skills of disengaging from our own existential concerns in order to better understand the phenomena we are observing;

(3) the ability to place the phenomenon confronting us in the context of the social and economic as well as in the context of the individual and family (e.g. the links between unemployment and depression or unemployment and child battering).

These interpretive skills would form an invaluable aid in the process of assessment of problems and needs and might well improve the social worker's ability to make appropriate decisions in relation to clients.

An understanding of social theory and social structure may also lead to an improved understanding by the social worker of social problem causation and the role and functions of social welfare. As we have seen in Chapter 6, a critical assessment of social theory may lead to a clearer definition of social problem causation and of the role of the social welfare worker in problem resolution or mitigation.

A critical and careful assessment of consensus and order theories of society may, for instance, lead the practitioner to regard as a theoretical problematic the causation of social problems. Poverty, ill health, delinquency, etc. may, on the one hand, be regarded as deviations from the harmonious and consensual workings of the major society. They may, on the other, be seen as manifestations of the conflict of values and interests which characterize relationships between different social groups or different social classes.

A careful and ongoing analysis at the micro- as well as at the macro-level will hopefully have implications for when and how the social worker acts as therapist, advocate, controller, or facilitator and will also heighten awareness of what sort of actions might be encouraged or constrained by state welfare agencies.

As we have also seen, micro sociology may also have an impact on helping social workers to practise in conscious and reflective ways (see pp. 163–7).

The advantages of closer association between sociology and

social work at a theoretical and at a practical level might also be seen as working to the benefit of sociology. Put quite bluntly, the practice of social work provides an arena to test the utility of sociological theory. In the final analysis, I would wish to argue, tests of sociological explanations are not so much tests of abstract truth as tests of social utility. How useful is this or that sociological explanation? Social work, confronting as it does, for example, the issues of behaviours and attitudes said to be associated with social class, gender, the results of institutionalization, the effects of stigma, and so on, provides a wonderful arena for the testing of sociological theory.

Social work practice might provide an important context in which to test or retest a number of the central hypotheses related to contemporary social life. For example,

- Is differential social class membership associated with different perceptions of control over people's lives, with different socialization processes, with different perceptions of the structure of society?
- Is the differential treatment of men and women discriminatory and, if so, is this discrimination entrenched through childhood socialization in the family and the education system?
- Can social work practice throw light on the argued effects of institutionalization and stigma in our dealings with the ill and handicapped?

Social work practice might almost be seen as a process of practical hermeneutics.

Both sociology and social work have much to gain from each other. Whether the problems associated with greater intellectual interpenetration are perceived as outweighing the advantages to both remains to be seen.

Bibliography

Addison, P. (1982), *The Road to 1945* (London: Quartet)

Allen, S. (ed.) (1974), *Conditions of Illusion* (London: Feminist Books)

Althusser, L. (1971), 'Ideology and ideological state apparatuses', in *Lenin and Philosophy and Other Essays* (London: New Left Books)

Bacon, R. and Eltis, W. A. (1976), *Britain's Economic Problem: Too Few Producers* (London: Macmillan)

Bailey, J. (1980), *Ideas and Intervention: Social Theory for Practice* (London: Routledge & Kegan Paul)

Bailey, R., and Brake, M. (eds) (1975), *Radical Social Work* (London: Edward Arnold)

Banks, O. (1981), *Faces of Feminism* (Oxford: Martin Robertson)

Baran, P. A., and Sweezy, P. M., (1968), *Monopoly Capital* (Harmondsworth: Penguin Books)

Barker, J. (1979), 'Social conscience and social policy', *Journal of Social Policy*, vol. 8, no. 2, pp. 177–206

Barker, R. (1978), *Political Ideas in Modern Britain* (London: Methuen)

Barnett, A. (1984), 'Beyond consensus', *New Socialist*, no. 18, pp. 33–5

Barnett, S. (1896), *What is Toynbee Hall?* (London: Toynbee Hall)

Barratt-Brown, M. (1972), *From Labourism to Socialism* (Leeds: Spokesman Books)

Bean, P., and MacPherson, S. (eds) (1983), *Approaches to Welfare* (London: Routledge & Kegan Paul)

Bell, D. (1960), *The End of Ideology* (New York: Free Press)

Bellaby, P. (1977), *The Sociology of Comprehensive Schooling* (London: Methuen)

Benn, C., and Simon, B. (1972), *Half-Way There* (Harmondsworth: Penguin Books)

Bessell, R. (1970), *Introduction to Social Work* (London: Batsford)

Bettelheim, B. (1969), *The Children of the Dream* (London: Thames & Hudson)

Beveridge, Sir W. (1942), *Social Insurance and Allied Services*, Cmnd 6404 (London: HMSO)

Blackburn, R. (ed.) (1972), *Ideology in the Social Sciences* (London: Fontana)

Blackburn, R. (1972), 'The new capitalism', in R. Blackburn (ed.) (1972)

Bolger, S., Corrigan, Paul, Docking, J., Frost, N. (1981), *Towards Socialist Welfare Work* (London: Macmillan)

Bosanquet, N. (1983), *After the New Right* (London: Heinemann)

Bowlby, J. (1953), *Child Care and the Growth of Love* (Harmondsworth: Penguin Books)

Boyson, R. (ed.) (1971), *Down with the Poor* (London: Churchill Press)

Brake, M., and Bailey, R. (eds) (1980), *Radical Social Work and Practice* (London: Edward Arnold)

Bremner, M. (1968), *Dependency and the Family* (London: Institute of Economic Affairs)

Bremner, R. (1974), 'Shifting attitudes', in P. E. Weinberger (ed.) (1974)

Brittain, V. (1953), *Lady into Woman* (London: Dakers)

Bronfenbrenner, U. (1974), *Two Worlds of Childhood* (Harmondsworth: Penguin Books)

Brook, E., and Davis, A. (1985), *Women, the Family and Social Work* (London: Tavistock)

Brown, G. W., and Harris, T. (1978), *Social Origins of Depression* (London: Tavistock)

Brown, M. (1976), *Introduction to Social Administration* (London: Hutchinson)

Case Con Collective (1970), 'Case Con manifesto', *Case-Con*, 1

Cawson, A. (1982), *Corporatism and Welfare* (London: Heinemann)

Chesler, P. (1972), *Women and Madness* (New York: Doubleday)

Clarke, J. (1980), 'Social Democratic delinquents and Fabian families', in M. Fitzgerald *et al.* (eds), *Permissiveness and Control* (London: Macmillan)

Coates, K., and Silburn, R. (1970), *Poverty, the Forgotten Englishman* (Harmondsworth: Penguin Books)

Coates, K. and Silburn, R. (1983), *Poverty, the Forgotten Englishman* (2nd edn) (Leeds: Spokesman Books)

Cohen, S. (1975), 'It's alright for you to talk: political and sociological manifestos for social work action', in R. Bailey and M. Brake (eds) (1975)

Comer, L. (1971), *The Myth of Motherhood* (Leeds: Spokesman Pamphlets)

Conservative Party (1979), *Conservative Manifesto: 1979* (London: Conservative Central Office)

Conservative Party (1983), *Conservative Manifesto: 1983* (London: Conservative Central Office)

Corrigan, Paul (1975), 'Community work and political struggle', in P. Leonard (ed.) (1975), *The Sociology of Community Action* (Keele: University of Keele)

Corrigan, Paul (1977), 'The welfare state as an arena for class struggle', *Marxism Today* (March), pp. 87–93

Corrigan, Paul (1979), 'Popular consciousness and social democracy', *Marxism Today* (December), pp. 14–17

Corrigan, Paul, and Leonard, P. (1978), *Social Work Practice under Capitalism* (London: Macmillan)

Corrigan, Philip (ed.) (1980), *Capitalism, State Formation and Marxist Theory* (London: Quartet)

Cowley, J., Kaye, A., Mayo, M., and Thompson, M. (eds) (1977), *Community or Class Struggle* (London: Stage One Publishing)

Cox, A., and Mead, M. (eds) (1975), *A Sociology of Medical Practice* (London: Collier-Macmillan)

Craig, G., Derricourt, N., and Loney, M. (eds) (1982), *Community Work and the State* (London: Routledge & Kegan Paul)

Crosland, C. A. R. (1952), 'The transition from capitalism', in R. H. S. Crossman (ed.) (1952)

Crosland, C. A. R. (1956), *The Future of Socialism* (London: Jonathan Cape)

Crosland, C. A. R. (1974), *Socialism Now* (London: Jonathan Cape)

Crosland, S. (1982), *Tony Crosland* (London: Jonathan Cape)

Crossman, R. H. S. (1950), *Socialist Values in a Changing Society* (London: Fabian Society)

Crossman, R. H. S. (ed.) (1952), *New Fabian Essays* (London: Turnstile Press)

Crossman, R. H. S. (1975), *Diaries of a Cabinet Minister: Volume 1* (London: Jonathan Cape)

Curtis, M. (1946), *Report of the Committee on the Care of Children*, Cmnd 6922 (London: HMSO)

Dale, J., and Foster, P. (1986) *Feminists and State Welfare* (London: Routledge & Kegan Paul)

Dalton, K. (1969), *The Menstrual Cycle* (Harmondsworth: Penguin Books)

Deem, R. (1978), *Women and Schooling* (London: Routledge & Kegan Paul)

Delamont, S. (1980) *Sex Roles and the School* (London: Methuen)

Department of Health and Social Security (1986), *The Reform of Social Security* (London: HMSO)

Dicey, A. V. (1962), *Law and Public Opinion in England* (London: Macmillan) (1st edn published in 1914)

Donzelot, J. (1980), *The Policing of Families* (London: Hutchinson)

Doyal, L. (1983), *The Political Economy of Health* (London: Pluto Press)

Dunning, E. A., and Hopper, E. I. (1966), 'Industrialisation and the problem of convergence: a critical note', *Sociological Review*, vol. 14, no. 2, pp. 163–86

Ehrenreich, B., and English, D. (1979), *For Her Own Good* (London: Pluto Press)

Elis Thomas, D. (1985), Unpublished paper delivered at British Association of Social Workers National Conference, at University College of Swansea

Fenwick, I. G. K. (1976), *The Comprehensive School: 1940–1970* (London: Methuen)

Finch, J., and Groves, D. (eds) (1983), *Labour of Love* (London: Routledge & Kegan Paul)

Foot, M. (1975), *Aneurin Bevan: 1945–1960* (London: Paladin)

Friedman, M. (1962), *Capitalism and Freedom* (Chicago: Chicago University Press)

Friedman, M., and Friedman, R. (1980), *Free to Choose* (Harmondsworth: Penguin Books)

Galbraith, J. K. (1963), *American Capitalism* (Harmondsworth: Penguin Books)

Galbraith, J. K. (1972), *The New Industrial Society* (Harmondsworth: Penguin Books)

Gamble, A. (1979), 'The decline of the Conservative Party', *Marxism Today* (November), pp. 6–12

Gamble, A. (1980), 'Thatcher: make or break', *Marxism Today* (November), pp. 14–19

Gamble, A. (1985), 'Smashing the state: Thatcher's radical crusade', *Marxism Today* (June), pp. 21–6

George, V. (1973), *Social Security and Society* (London: Routledge & Kegan Paul)

George, V., and Wilding, P. (1976), *Ideology and Social Welfare* (London: Routledge & Kegan Paul)

George, V., and Wilding, P. (1984), *The Impact of Social Policy* (London: Routledge & Kegan Paul)

George, V., and Wilding, P. (1985), *Ideology and Social Welfare* (revised edn) (London: Routledge & Kegan Paul)

Gieve, K. (1974), 'The independence demand', in S. Allen (ed.) (1974)

Ginsburg, N. (1979), *Class, Capital and Social Policy* (London: Macmillan)

Gold, D. A., Lo, C. Y., and Wright, E. O. (1975), 'Recent developments in Marxist theories of the state', *Monthly Review* (New York) vol. 27, no. 5

Goldthorpe, J. H. (1962), 'The development of Social Policy in England', *Transactions of the 5th World Congress of Sociology*

Gough, I. (1975), 'State expenditure in advanced capitalism', *New Left Review*, vol. 92, pp. 53–92

Gough, I. (1979), *The Political Economy of the Welfare State* (London: Macmillan)

Gove, W. R., and Tudor, J. F. (1973), 'Adult sex roles and mental illness', *American Journal of Sociology*, vol. 78, pp. 812–35

Gregg, P. (1967), *The welfare state: an economic and social history of Great Britain from 1945 to the present day* (London: Harrap)

Griffiths, B. (1983), *The Moral Basis of the Market Economy* (London: Conservative Political Centre)

Gulbenkian Foundation (1968), *Community Work and Social Change* (London: Longmans)

Habermas, J. (1976), *Legitimation Crisis* (London: Heinemann)

Hall, Penelope (1952), *The Social Services of Modern England* (London: Routledge & Kegan Paul)

Hall, Phoebe, Land, H., Parker, R., and Webb, A. (1978), *Change, Choice and Conflict in Social Policy* (London: Heinemann)

Hall, S. (1979), 'The great moving right show', *Marxism Today* (January), pp. 14–20

Hall, S., Critcher, C., Jefferson, T., Clarke, J., and Roberts, B. (1979), *Policing the Crisis* (London: Macmillan)

Halmos, P. (1965), *The Faith of the Counsellors* (London: Constable)

Halmos, P. (1978), *The Personal and the Political* (London: Hutchinson)

Halsey, A. H., Heath, A. F., and Ridge, J. M. (1980), *Origins and Destinations* (Oxford: Oxford University Press)

Handler, J. (1973), *The Coercive Social Worker* (Chicago: Rand McNally)

Harris, L. (1984), 'State and economy in the Second World War', in McLennan, G., Held, D. and Hall S. (eds) (1984), *State and Society in Contemporary Britain* (Cambridge: Polity Press)

Harris, R. (1971), *Choice in Welfare* (London: Institute of Economic Affairs)

Harris, R., and Seldon, A. (1979), *Overruled on Welfare* (London: Institute of Economic Affairs)

Harrison, R. (1965), *Before the Socialists* (London: Routledge & Kegan Paul)

Hart, J. T. (1975), 'The inverse care law', in A. Cox and M. Mead (eds) (1975)

Hartman, H. (ed.) (1981), *The Unhappy Marriage of Marxism and Feminism* (London: Pluto Press)

Hayek, F. A. (1944), *The Road to Serfdom* (London: Routledge & Kegan Paul)

Hayek, F. A. (1949), *Individualism and the Economic Order* (London: Routledge & Kegan Paul)

Hayek, F. A. (1960), *The Constitution of Liberty* (London: Routledge & Kegan Paul)

Hayek, F. A. (1973), *Law, Legislation and Liberty*, Vol. 1 (London: Routledge & Kegan Paul)

Hayek, F. A. (1976), *Law, Legislation and Liberty*, Vol. 2 (London: Routledge & Kegan Paul)

Hayek, F. A. (1979), *Law, Legislation and Liberty*, Vol. 3 (London: Routledge & Kegan Paul)

Hayek, F. A. (1980), *1980s Unemployment and the Unions* (London: Institute of Economic Affairs)

Held, D. (ed.) (1982), *Classes, Power and Conflict* (London: Macmillan)

Held, D., *et al.* (eds) (1983), *States and Societies* (Oxford: Martin Robertson)

Heraud, B. (1970), *Sociology and Social Work* (Oxford: Pergamon Press)

Hobsbawm, E. (1964), *Labouring Men* (London: Weidenfeld & Nicolson)

Hollingshead, A., and Redlich, R. C. (1958), *Social Class and Mental Illness* (New York: John Wiley)

Holman, R. (1978), *Poverty: Explanations of Social Deprivation* (Oxford: Martin Robertson)

Home Office (1965), *The Child, the Family and the Young Offender*, Cmnd 2742 (London: HMSO)

Home Office (1968), *Children in Trouble*, Cmnd 3601 (London: HMSO)

Howe, Sir G. (1983), 'Agenda for liberal Conservatism', *Journal of Economic Affairs* (January)

Jenkins, Roy (1972), *What Matters Now* (London: Fontana).

Jessop, Bob (1977), 'Recent theories of the capitalist state', *Cambridge Journal of Economics*, vol. 1, pp. 353–73

Jessop, Bob (1980), 'The transformation of the state in post-war Britain', in R. Scase (ed.) (1980)

Jones, Catherine, and Stevenson, J. (1983), *Yearbook of Social Policy, 1982* (London: Routledge & Kegan Paul)

Jones, Chris (1983), *State Social Work and the Working Class* (London: Macmillan)

Jones, H. (1971), *Crime in a Changing Society* (Harmondsworth: Penguin Books)

Jones, H. (ed.) (1981), *Society against Crime* (Harmondsworth: Penguin Books)

Jordan, B. (1974), *Poor Parents* (London: Routledge & Kegan Paul)

Jordan, B. (1981), *Automatic Poverty* (London: Routledge & Kegan Paul)

Jordan, B., and Parton, N. (1983), *The Political Dimensions of Social Work* (Oxford: Blackwell)

Joseph, Sir K. (1972), 'The cycle of deprivation', Speech delivered to a conference of the Pre-School Play Association

Joseph, Sir K. (1976), *Stranded on the Middle Ground* (London: Centre for Policy Studies)

Joseph, Sir K., and Sumption, J. (1979), *Equality* (London: John Murray)

Kerr, C., Dunlop, J. T., Harbison, F. H., Myers, C. A. (1962), *Industrialism and Industrial Man* (London: Heinemann)

Kincaid, J. (1973), *Poverty and Equality in Britain* (Harmondsworth: Penguin Books)

King, A. (ed.) (1969), *The British Prime Minister* (London: Macmillan)

Kinnock, N. (1986), *The Future of Socialism* (London: Fabian Society)

Klein, R. (1974), *Social Policy and Public Expenditure* (London: Centre for Studies in Social Policy)

Kogan, M. (1971), *The Politics of Education* (Harmondsworth: Penguin Books)

Kuenstler, P. (1961), *Community Organisation in Great Britain* (London: Faber)

Labour Party (1964), *Let's Go with Labour for the New Britain* (London: Labour Party)

Labour Party Research Department (1985), *Breaking the Nation* (London: Pluto Press/New Socialist)

Lafitte, F. (1962), *Social Policy in a Free Society* (Birmingham: University of Birmingham)

Laing, R. D. (1975), *The Divided Self* (Harmondsworth: Penguin Books)

Laing, R. D., and Esterson, A. (1974), *Sanity, Madness and the Family* (Harmondsworth: Penguin Books)

Land, H. (1978), 'Who cares for the family?', *Journal of Social policy*, vol. 7, pp. 257–84

Laski, H. J. (1934), *The State in Theory and Practice* (London: Allen & Unwin)

Lawson, N. (1981), *The New Conservatism* (London: Conservative Political Centre)

Leeson, J., and Gray, J. (1978), *Women and Medicine* (London: Tavistock)

LeGrand, J. (1982), *The Strategy of Equality* (London: Allen & Unwin)

LeGrand, J., and Robinson, R. (eds) (1984), *Privatisation and the Welfare State* (London: Allen & Unwin)

Lejeune, A. (ed.) (1970), *Enoch Powell* (London: Stacey)

Leonard, P. (1975), 'Towards a paradigm for radical practice', in R. Bailey and M. Brake (eds) (1975)

Leonard, P. (1979), 'Restructuring the welfare state', *Marxism Today* (December), pp. 7–13

Leonard, P. (1983), 'Marxism, the individual and the welfare state', in P. Bean and S. MacPherson (eds) (1983)

Lewis, J. (1973), 'Beyond suffrage: English feminism in the 1920s', *The Maryland Historian*, no. 6. pp. 1–17

Lewis, O. (1961), *The Children of Sanchez* (New York: Random House)

Lidbetter, E. J. (1933), *Heredity and the Social Problem Group* (London: Edward Arnold)

London Edinburgh Weekend Return Group (1980), *In and against the State* (London: Pluto Press)

Loney, M. (1983), *Community against Government* (London: Heinemann)

Loney, M., Boswell, D., and Clarke, J. (1984), *Social Policy and Social Welfare* (Milton Keynes: Open University Press)

Longford, F. (1966), *Crime: a Challenge to us all* (London: Labour Party)

McIntosh, M. (1984), 'The family, regulation and the public sphere', in G. McLennan, D. Held, S. Hall (eds) (1984), *State and Society in Contemporary Britain* (Cambridge: Polity Press)

Mack, J., and Lansley, S. (1985), *Poor Britain* (London: Allen & Unwin)

McLennan, G., Held, D., and Hall, S. (eds) (1983), *States and Societies* (Cambridge: Polity Press)

McLennan, G., Held, D., and Hall, S. (1984), *The Idea of the Modern State* (Milton Keynes: Open University Press)

McLeod, I., and Powell, J. E. (1952), *The Social Services* (London: Conservative Political Centre)

Mandel, E. (1968), *Marxist Economic Theory* (London: Merlin)

Marshall, T. H. (1963), 'Citizenship and social class', in *Sociology at the Crossroads* (London: Heinemann)

Marshall, T. H. (1965), *Social Policy* (London: Hutchinson)

Marshall, T. H. (1975), *Social Policy* (revised edn) (London: Hutchinson)

Martin, A. (1913), 'The mother and social reform', in *Married Women and Social Reform*, in the journal *Nineteenth Century*

Marwick, A. (1974), *War and Social Change in the Twentieth Century* (London: Macmillan)

Marwick, A. (1980), *Class, Image and Reality in Britain, France and the USA since 1930* (London: Collins)

Marwick, A. (1982), *British Society since 1945* (Harmondsworth: Penguin Books)

Marx, K. (1967), *Capital* (London: Dent)

Marx, K. (1973), 'The Eighteenth Brumaire of Louis Bonaparte', in D. Fernbach (ed.) (1973) *Marx: Surveys from Exile* (Harmondsworth: Penguin Books)

Marx, K., and Engels, F. (1967), *The Communist Manifesto* (Harmondsworth: Penguin Books)

Maude, A. (1977), *The Right Approach to the Economy* (London: Conservative Political Centre)

Meyer, P. (1983), *The Child and the State* (Cambridge: Cambridge University Press)

Middlemas, K. (1979), *Politics in Industrial Society* (London: André Deutsch)

Miliband, R. (1969), *The State in Capitalist Society* (London: Weidenfeld & Nicolson)

Miliband, R. (1978), *Marxism and Politics* (Oxford: Oxford University Press)

Miliband, R. (1982), *Capitalist Democracy in Britain* (Oxford: Oxford University Press)

Mills, C. Wright (1943), 'The professional ideology of social pathologists', *American Journal of Sociology*, vol. 49

Mills, C. Wright (1959), *The Sociological Imagination* (Oxford: Oxford University Press)

Mishra, R. (1975), 'Marx and welfare', *Sociological Review*, vol. 23, no. 2, pp. 287–313

Mishra, R. (1981), *Society and Social Policy* (London: Macmillan)

Mishra, R. (1984), *The Welfare State in Crisis* (Brighton: Wheatsheaf)

Mount, F. (1982), *The Subversive Family* (London: Jonathan Cape)

Munday, B. (1972), 'What is happening to social work students?', *Social Work Today*, vol. 3, no. 6

Novarra, V. (1980), *Women's Work, Men's Work: the Ambivalence of Equality* (London: Boyars)

NSPCC (1984), 'An overview of the research on the effects of unemployment on the family with particular reference to child abuse', *Information Briefing*, no. 1 (London: NSPCC)

Oakley, A. (1974), *The Sociology of Housework* (Oxford: Martin Robertson)

O'Connor, J. (1973), *The Fiscal Crisis of the State* (New York: St Martin's Press)

Offe, C. (1982), 'Some contradictions of the modern welfare state', *Critical Social Policy*, vol. 2, no. 2, pp. 7–16

Offe, C. (1984), *Contradictions of the Welfare State* (London: Hutchinson)

Offe, C., and Ronge, V. (1975), 'Theses on the theory of the state', *New German Critique*, vol. 6, pp. 139–47

O'Higgins, M. (1983), 'Rolling back the welfare state', in C. Jones, and J. Stevenson (eds) (1983)

Olsen, M. R. (ed.) (1984), *Social Work and Mental Health* (London: Tavistock)

Packman, J. (1975), *The Child's Generation* (Oxford: Basil Blackwell and Martin Robertson)

Parker, J. (1975), *Social Policy and Citizenship* (London: Macmillan)

Parkinson, M. (1970), *The Labour Party and the Organisation of Secondary Education 1918–65* (London: Routledge & Kegan Paul)

Parry, N., and Parry, J. (1979), 'Social work, professionalism and the state', in N. Parry, M. Rustin and C. Satyamurti (1979)

Parry, N., Rustin, M., and Satyamurti, C. (eds) (1979), *Social Work, Welfare and the State* (London: Edward Arnold)

Parton, N., and Thomas, T. (1983), 'Child abuse and citizenship', in B. Jordan and N. Parton (eds) (1983)

Pascall, G. (1983), 'Women and social welfare', in P. Bean and S. MacPherson (eds) (1983)

Pearce, F. (1973), 'The British road to incorporation', *The Writing on the Wall*, vol. 2

Pearson, G. (1973), 'Social work as the privatised solution to public ills', *British Journal of Social Work*, vol. 3, no. 2, pp. 209–23

Philp, A. F. (1963), *Family Failure* (London: Faber)

Poulantzas, N. (1972), 'The problem of the capitalist state', in R. Blackburn (ed.) (1972)

Poulantzas, N. (1973), *Political Power and Social Classes* (London: New Left Books)

Poulantzas, N. (1975), *Classes in Contemporary Society* (London: New Left Books)

Powell, J. E. (1966), *Medicine and Politics* (London: Pitman)

Powell, J. E. (1969), *Freedom and Reality* (London: Elliot Rightway Books)

Powell, J. E. (1972), *Still to Decide* (London: Elliot Rightway Books)

Rapoport, R., Rapoport, N., and Strelitz, Z. (1977), *Fathers, Mothers and Others* (London: Routledge & Kegan Paul)

Redwood, J., and Hatch, J. (1982), *Controlling Public Industries* (Oxford: Basic Blackwell)

Reynolds, D., and Sullivan, M. (1986), *The Comprehensive Experiment* (Brighton: Falmer Press)

Riddell, P. (1983), *The Thatcher Government* (Oxford: Martin Robertson)

Robbins, Lord (1963), *Report on Higher Education*, Cmnd 2514 (London: HMSO)

Robertson, D. J., and Hunter, L. C. (1970), *Labour Market Issues of the 1970s* (Edinburgh: Oliver & Boyd)

Robertson, J. (1962), *Hospitals and Children* (London: Gollancz)

Robson, W. (1976), *Welfare State and Welfare Society* (London: Allen & Unwin)

Rodgers, B. (1969), *The Battle Against Poverty* (London: Routledge & Kegan Paul)

Roof, M. (1972), *A Hundred Years of Family Welfare* (London: Michael Joseph)

Rubinstein, D., and Simon, B. (1973), *The Evolution of the Comprehensive School 1926–1972* (London: Routledge & Kegan Paul)

Rutter, M. (1975), *Maternal Deprivation Reassessed* (Harmondsworth: Penguin Books)

Rutter, M., and Madge, N. (1977), *Cycles of Disadvantage* (London: Heinemann)

Ryan, W. (1971), *Blaming the Victim* (New York: Random House)

Sainsbury, E. (1977), *The Personal Social Services* (London: Pitman)

Saville, J. (1957), 'The welfare state: an historical approach', *New Reasoner*, vol. 3

Scase, R. (ed.) (1980), *The State in Western Europe* (London: Croom Helm)

Scheff, T. (1968), *Being Mentally Ill: a Sociological Theory* (London: Weidenfeld & Nicolson)

Schott, K. (1982), 'The use of Keynesian economics: Britain 1940–64', *Economy and Society*, vol. 11, no. 3 (reproduced in G. McLennan, D. Held and S. Hall (eds), 1983)

Seebohm, F., Sir (1968), *Report of the Committee on Local Authority and Allied Personal Social Services*, Cmnd 3703 (London: HMSO)

Seed, P. (1973), *The Expansion of Social Work in Britain* (London: Routledge & Kegan Paul)

Seldon, A. (1967), *Taxation and Welfare* (London: Institute of Economic Affairs)

Seldon, A. (1977), *Charge* (London: Temple Smith)

Seldon, A. (1981), *Wither the Welfare State* (London: Institute of Economic Affairs)

Sked, A., and Cook, C. (1979), *Post War Britain: a Political History* (Harmondsworth: Penguin Books)

Slack, K. (1966), *Social Administration and the Citizen* (London: Michael Joseph)

Steadman Jones, G. (1971), *Outcast London* (Oxford: Oxford University Press)

Sullivan, M. (1984), 'The crisis in welfare?', Unpublished paper presented to School of Social Studies Colloqium, University College of Swansea

Tawney, R. H. (1964), *The Radical Tradition* (Harmondsworth: Penguin Books)

Taylor-Gooby, P. (1985), *Public Opinion, Ideology and State Welfare* (London: Routledge & Kegan Paul)

Taylor-Gooby, P., and Dale, J. (1981), *Social Theory and Social Welfare* (London: Edward Arnold)

Thatcher, M. (1977), *Let Our Children Grow Tall* (London: Centre for Policy Studies)

Thompson, E. P. (1963), *The Making of the English Working Class* (London: Gollancz)

Thompson, G. (1984), 'Rolling back the state: economic intervention 1975–82', in G. McLennan, D. Held, and S. Hall, *State and Society in Contemporary Britain* (Cambridge: Polity Press)

Timms, N. (1967), *Psychiatric Social Work in Great Britain* (London: Routledge & Kegan Paul)

Timms, N., and Watson, D. (eds) (1976), *Talking about Welfare* (London: Routledge & Kegan Paul)

Titmuss, R. (1963), *Essays on the Welfare State* (London: Allen & Unwin)

Townsend, P. (1974), 'The cycle of deprivation: the history of a confused thesis', in Thomas, J. (ed.) (1974) *The Cycle of Deprivation* (Birmingham: BASW Publications)

Townsend, P. (1979), *Poverty in the UK* (Harmondsworth: Penguin Books)

Townsend, P., and Abel-Smith, B. (1965), *The Poor and the Poorest* (London: Bell)

Townsend, P., and Davidson, N. (1982), *Inequalities in Health* (Harmondsworth: Penguin Books)

Valentine, C. A. (1968), *Culture and Poverty* (Chicago: Chicago University Press)

Walton, R. (1975), *Women in Social Work* (London: Routledge & Kegan Paul)

Weinberger, P. E. (ed.) (1974), *Perspectives on Social Welfare* (New York: Macmillan)

Whetham, W. C. D. (1909), *The Family and the Nation* (London: Longman and Green)

Wilensky, H. L., and Lebaux, C. N. (1965), *Industrial Society and Social Welfare* (New York: Free Press)

Willcocks, A. (1967), *The Creation of the National Health Service* (London: Routledge & Kegan Paul)

Williams, F. (1969), 'A Prime Minister remembers', in A. King (ed.) (1969)

Williams, G. A. (1968), *Artisans and Sans Coulottes* (London: Edward Arnold)

Williams, S. (1981), *Politics Is for People* (Harmondsworth: Penguin Books)

Wilson, E. (1977), *Women and the Welfare State* (London: Tavistock)

Wilson, E. (1980), 'Feminism and social work', in M. Brake and R. Bailey (eds) (1980)

Wilson, E. (1981), *Only Half Way to Paradise* (London: Tavistock)

Wilson, H., and Herbert, G. (1978), *Parenting in the Inner City* (London: Routledge & Kegan Paul)

Woodroofe, K. (1971), *From Charity to Social Work* (London: Routledge & Kegan Paul)

Wooton, B. (1959), *Social Science and Social Pathology* (London: Allen & Unwin)

Name Index

Addison, P. 5
Althusser, L. 49–50, 125, 149

Bacon, R. and Eltis, W. A. 141
Bailey, J. 168–9, 170
Banks, O. 75
Baran, P. and Sweezy, P. 46, 51, 52, 83, 149
Barker, J. 107–8
Barker, P. 6
Barnett, A. 18
Barratt-Brown, M. 46, 49
Bellaby, P. 51, 56, 144
Bettelhelm, B. 165
Beveridge, Sir, W. 1
Blackburn, R. 135
Bolger, S. 119, 122–3, 153, 155
Bowlby, J. 126, 165
Boyson, R. 22, 56, 58, 93–4, 96–7, 145
Bremner, R. 158
Brittain, V. 77
Bronfenbrenner, U. 165
Brook, E. and Davis, A. 124, 126–7, 164
Brown, G. W. and Harris, T. 166
Brown, M. 68

Cawson, A. 38, 145
Clarke, J. 122–3
Coates, K. and Silburn, R. 157, 161, 163
Cohen, S. 123, 168
Comer, L. 127
Corrigan, Paul 117
Corrigan, Paul and Leonard, P. 117, 123, 152
Craig, G., Derricourt, N. and Loney, M. 154
Crosland, C. A. R. 30, 33, 35, 36, 72, 73–4, 84, 109–10, 132, 133

Crosland, S. 134
Crossman, R. H. 30, 41, 133

Dale, J. and Foster, P. 62, 75–6
Dalton, K. 167
Deem, R. 91
Delamont, S. 91
Dicey, A. 93
Donzelot, J. 92, 121, 128
Doyal, L. 136
Dunning, E. and Hopper, E. 40, 41, 77–8

Ehrenreich, B. and English, D. 126, 165
Elis Thomas, D. 3

Fenwick, I. G. K. 15, 132
Field, F. 14
Finch, J. and Groves, D. 127
Foot, M. 15
Friedman, M. 17, 56, 57, 58, 60, 128–9

Galbraith, J. K. 40–1, 42, 43, 78, 140, 143, 147
Gamble, A. 21
George, V 13, 67, 103
George, V and Wilding, P. 3, 34–5, 47, 59, 60, 96, 136, 147
Gieve, K. 125
Ginsburg, N. 48, 51, 86, 89
Gold, D., Lo, C. and Wright, E. 45
Goldthorpe, J. 139, 140
Gough, I. 3, 48, 51, 56, 85–6, 90, 120, 153
Gove, W. R. and Tudor, J. F. 167
Griffiths, B. 23
Gregg, P. 67

Hall, P. 64, 106–7, 110–11

188

Hall, P., Land, H., Parker, R. and Webb, A. 13, 14
Hall, S. 2, 21
Halmos, P. 170
Halsey, A. H., Heath, A. F. and Ridge, J. M. 136, 147, 160
Handler, J. 92
Harris, L. 4, 8
Harris, R. and Seldon, A. 56, 58, 142
Hayek, F. 17, 30, 56, 57, 58, 93, 96–7, 128–9, 141
Held, D. 13
Heraud, B. 161, 171
Hollingshead, A. and Redlich, R. 166
Holman, R. 157, 160, 161
Howe, Sir. G. 22

Jenkins, R. 111, 152
Jessop, B. 9, 30, 45, 145
Jones, C. 116, 119, 120, 123, 152, 155
Jordan, B. 156, 157
Joseph, K. 17, 22, 24, 111, 152, 156
Joseph, K. and Sumption, J. 18, 56

Kerr, C. 40, 41, 42, 77, 139, 147
Kincaid, J. 14
Kinnock, N. 98
Klein, R. 142
Kogan, M. 15

Labour Party Research Department 24, 25
Laing, R. 167
Land, H. 14
Laski, H. 50
Lawson, N. 21
Leeson, J. and Gray, J. 167
LeGrand, J. 136
LeGrand, J. and Robinson, R. 25
Leonard, P. 2, 21, 120, 123
Lewis, O. 156, 159
London Edinburgh Weekend Return Group 3, 155
Loney, M. 62, 77, 125, 153, 154, 156

McIntosh, M. 127
McLennan, G., Held, D. and Hall, S. 13
Mack, J. and Lansley, S. 156, 163
Mandel, E. 46, 49, 51, 83, 149

Marshall, T. H. 2, 31–2, 36, 65, 70–2, 109–10, 132, 146
Marwick, A. 1, 4, 37
Marx, K. 45, 82, 83
Maude, A. 24
Meyer, P. 128
Middlemas, K. 10
Miliband, R. 45, 47, 48, 55
Mills, C. Wright ix, 155, 173
Mishra, R. 2, 3, 42, 80, 82
Mount, F. 145
Munday, B. 168

Novarra, V. 76
N.S.P.C.C. 157

Oakley, A. 167
O'Connor, J. 46, 49, 52, 56, 84–5, 88–9, 148, 172
Offe, C. 51, 87, 152
Offe, C. and Ronge, V. 47, 51
O'Higgins, M. 26–7
Olsen, M. R. 166

Packman, J. 152
Parkinson, M. 15, 68
Parker, J. 70
Parry, N. 104
Parton, N. and Thomas, T. 157
Pascall, G. 125
Pearson, G. 152
Philp, A. F. 158
Poulantzas, N. 45, 48, 50
Powell, E. 17, 22, 56, 57, 58, 59, 84, 95

Rapoport, R., Rapoport, R. and Strelitz, Z. 165
Redwood, J. and Hatch, J. 24
Reynolds, D. and Sullivan, M. 132, 134, 144
Riddell, P. 19, 21, 38
Robbins, Lord 2
Robertson, D. J. and Hunter, L. C. 12
Robertson, J. 165
Robson, W. 66, 136
Rodgers, B. 67–8
Roof, M. 65
Rubinstein, D. and Simon, B. (1973) 5, 15, 68, 132

Rutter, M. 165
Rutter, M. and Madge, N. 157
Ryan, W. 157

Saville, J. 46, 49, 50, 51, 84, 88–9, 149, 172
Scase, R. 47
Scheff, T. 167
Schott, K. 35, 52
Seed, P. 104
Seldon, A. 22, 56, 58
Sked, A. and Cook, C. 1, 19, 37
Slack, K. 66, 69, 106, 136
Steadman Jones, G. 104–5, 113–15
Strachey, J. 33
Sullivan, M. 3, 20, 26

Tawney, R. H. 34
Taylor Gooby, P. 2, 3, 19, 25, 26, 39, 56, 133, 142, 143, 145, 146
Taylor Gooby, P. and Dale, J. 3
Thatcher, M. 129

Thompson, G. 24
Timms, N. 124
Titmuss, R. M. 107
Townsend, P. 157, 159, 160, 163
Townsend, P. and Abel Smith, B. 109, 135, 157
Townsend, P. and Davidson, N. 136, 147
Tudor Hart, J. 136

Valentine, C. A. 159

Walton, R. 124
Willcocks, A. 5
Willensky, H. and Lebaux, C. 78, 80, 112
Williams, S. 30
Wilson, E. 62, 75, 90–1, 117–18, 123, 124–5, 126, 164
Wilson, H. and Herbert, G. 160, 163
Woodroofe, K. 103–4
Wooton, B. 159

8

Subject Index

child rearing ideology 91–2, 126–7
community work 153–4
corporatism 19–21

economic management
  philosophy of 8–10
  planning and incorporation 10–12,
    38
education
  secondary schools 15
  higher education 15–16
  comprehensive education 68, 72, 79

feminism 74–6, 91–2, 97, 123–8

income maintenance
  post-war 13–15, 67–8, 79, 86, 89
  earnings related benefits 14, 79
industrial logic 31–3, 137–41
industrial society 40–5, 77–81
  see also 'industrial logic'

Keynesianism, failure of 37–8

Marxism 45–56, 82–92, 113–23
Marxist functionalism 48, 49–50,
  51–3, 82–5, 87–9

national health service 16–17

poverty
  and welfare 156–8
  and child abuse 157
  and social structure 158–61
    cultural explanations 159–60
  and sociological inquiry 158, 160–1
  and welfare systems 161–2

radical right 56–61, 92–7, 128–9
reformism 29–40, 62–77, 106–11

social work
  before the Welfare State 103–5
  postwar 105–6
  development and functions of
    106–29
  and philanthropy 103–4
  and social unrest 104, 113–15
  and the growth of social conscience
    107–10
  and the Children and Young
    Persons Acts 107–8, 120–2
  and reorganization 108–9, 152–3
  and amelioration 110–11
  and integration 112–13
  and containment 115–16, 118–19,
    120, 147–8
  and rehabilitation 116, 120
  as capitalist fraud 116–17
  and social democracy 117, 120
  and class struggle 117–18
  and feminism 123–8
  and women's role 124–7
  and the radical right 128–9
  and poverty 156–64
  and the family 164–6
  and mental health 166–7
sociology
  and social welfare systems 161–2
  and social work practice 163–7
state
  reformist views 29–39
  industrial state views 40–5
  marxist views 45–56
  radical right views 56–61
  transformation of 30–2, 40–1, 46–7,
    57–8
  authority of 32–3, 41, 47–8, 57–8
  and government 33–4, 41–2, 48–9,
    58–9
  role and function of 34–6, 42–3,
    49–51, 59–61

191

as handmaiden of capitalism 46, 47,
  148–9
as relatively autonomous 46, 48,
  151–4
as subservient to government 32–4,
  40–2, 57–8, 133–4, 139
state intervention
  war-time 4–5
  postwar 5–17
  consensus on 4–17, 33, 35, 37, 39,
    132
  conflict over 17–21, 39
  new conservatives and 21–3
  in the 1980s 23–8
  and social control 46–51
  and relative autonomy 47, 48–9,
    51–2

welfare
  social conscience thesis 64–9
  citizenship and 69–74
  feminism and 74–7, 91–2, 97
  and industrialism 77–81
  and capitalism 82–92
  and relative autonomy 85–6
  as handmaiden of capitalism 87–9
  as contradictory in nature 89–90
  as state tyranny 92–3
  as irresponsible 93–4
  as inefficient 95
welfare state
  development of 65–9, 70–2, 74–6,
    78–80, 82–7, 92–3
  aims and functions of 69, 72–4,
    76–7, 80–1, 87–90, 91–2, 93–5
  in the 1980s 97–102